The Private Pilot's Licence

David Ogilvy

A   don

First published 1987 by
A & C Black (Publishers) Limited
35 Bedford Row, London WC1R 4JH

© 1987 David Ogilvy

ISBN 0 7136 5588 7

British Library Cataloguing in Publication Data

Ogilvy, David, *1929–*
    The private pilot's licence.
    1. Airplanes—Piloting 2. Private
    flying
    I. Title
    629.132'5217   TL710

ISBN 0–7136–5588–7

Printed and bound in Great Britain by
the Bath Press Limited

Contents

Introduction

I hope that you will read this book from the time you think about learning to fly, as it may help guide you onto the right track to success. There are many points that you will not be told by your flying instructor. This is not a criticism of those who teach, for the material covered here is geared more to your approach and attitude to aviation than to the contents of the air and ground syllabus for the Private Pilot's Licence.

The Private Pilot's Licence is not a manual of instruction. It will not teach you to fly. There are specialist publications and organisations that fulfil those functions admirably. My aim is to give you tips from the sidelines, so that you can gain the maximum benefit from the facilities available. There are many ways in which you can learn more than just the basics by the way in which you use your time at the aerodrome, by listening and talking to other people, by careful observation of what other pilots are doing, by thinking why you may be told to tackle a problem in a particular way; and many more.

When you have gained your pilot's licence there are many opportunities open to you. The licence may be your sole and final target, which is quite acceptable, but there are numerous activities in which you can participate without obtaining any additional qualifications. Alternatively, you may wish to acquire added ratings and endorsements with the aim of becoming as highly qualified as possible. You may wish to fly purely for personal pleasure, or you may hope to use an aeroplane for business travelling. Soon you will discover which is for you, or you can learn to do both.

The primary purpose in my writing this book is to encourage you to learn to fly and, more importantly, to make the most of your licence once you have acquired it. Many newly qualified and some more experienced pilots seem to become lost in their searches for things to do. Some, alas, give up, which is a sad thought after spending time and money on learning to fly. There is no need to do this, or to lose heart, for there are many possible openings and outlets for you and your licence; there is something to suit everyone.

I remember as a young schoolboy being taken to the now defunct Woodley Aerodrome, near Reading, where I watched three Gipsy Moths, which impressed me greatly. I developed a strong desire to know more about light aeroplanes — not only to fly them, but to become involved in a wide range of associated aviation activities. Since then I have been a flying instructor, flying school manager, aerodrome manager, aircraft museum manager, private aircraft operator, racing pilot, organiser of flying events and a member of several related organisations. This is through neither skill nor ability, but through an irresistible desire to be involved, accompanied by the good luck to be in the right place at the right time. Light aviation can be almost a way of life, mixing its occasional frustrations with some of the greatest pleasures that any pastime can offer. Flying, with the engine well throttled back, on a calm summer evening during that final hour before dusk, with the long shadows growing almost visibly, is an exhilarating experience. Standing alone on an airfield at the end of a busy day's activities, looking across the deserted manoeuvring area that not long before was a hive of aeroplanes and people, is another. Each person must have his or her own sets of values, but as private flying offers so many alternatives, I cannot believe that there is any need for anyone to withdraw on grounds of boredom or lack of motivation. In the following chapters I hope to prove that point!

There are enormous gaps in my own knowledge and experience and I would be presumptuous to try to put forward only my own opinions. I have received welcome help from several friends who are able to offer expertise and their assistance has added significantly to this book. In particular, I wish to thank Bill Bowker of Bowker Air Services for information about self-launching motor gliders and John Fack of Pegasus Flight Training for some encouraging descriptions of flight in flex-wing microlights. Dr Alan Roscoe, an experienced specialist in aviation medicine, explains the recently revised medical requirements for the P.P.L. and offers a few words of guidance about health for the private pilot. Alfred Kingsnorth, a specialist broker in aviation insurance, has added a professional touch to Chapter 9. Finally, I should like to express thanks to John Ward, Chairman and Secretary of the General Aviation Safety Committee, who explains the importance of combining knowledge with common sense if flying is to remain as safe as it is — and, perhaps, become even safer.

I cannot overstress my main point, which is that private flying has much to offer. I offer no apology for making Chapter 7 the longest of all, for it aims to cover the various ways in which you can fly for personal pleasure; that, I feel, is the basis upon which the future growth of the movement must stand.

David Ogilvy

About the author
David Ogilvy has served as a P.P.L. examiner, a Chief Flying Instructor and Chief Instructor of the Air Schools Group. He organises flying displays for the Shuttleworth Collection in Bedfordshire, is an executive director of the British Light Aviation Centre and is a member of the Civil Aviation Authority's Standing Advisory Committee on Private Pilot Licensing, of the National Air Traffic Management Advisory Committee and of the General Aviation Safety Committee. He edits the magazine *Light Aviation* for the Aircraft Owners and Pilots Association

1
The World of Flying

What is private flying all about?

There may be be several questions which you wish to ask. What is private flying all about? Who goes in for it? Do I need to be strong or exceptionally fit? Do I learn with an individual, or do I go to a flying school? How do I know that I am going to the right person or place? Am I expected to know anything before I begin? Do I just turn up for a flight, pay and go away again, or do I need to put in more time and effort than that? How often should I fly? Does the weather matter very much? Do I need any special clothing or equipment? Will I meet other people who are beginners or will I be surrounded by experts who will make me feel inadequate? I know there are several rules of the road, including a speed limit, but does the air have a similar set of regulations that I must learn and obey? I am not too bad at finding my way round the country by road, but how do I do it in an aeroplane? And thinking of motoring, I do some of the maintenance on my own car, so what happens with aircraft? How do I know that the machine on which I am learning is safe to fly? How soon will I be able to go on my own and when will I be able to take a passenger with me? How do I know that I will not get too close to an airliner that is full of passengers? What choices do I have when I have obtained my licence? Is there more to learn? What restrictions are there? Do I continue flying the aircraft on which I have learned or do I go somewhere else to find an aeroplane? Is ownership practical or very expensive? Can I share a machine with a friend or with a group of people who have one in joint ownership? Are there any flying competitions or other activities in which I will be able to take part? What happens if I like flying so much that I want to go and earn my living from it?

The point of this book is to put you at ease on the whole subject of learning to fly and tell you what you can do when you have obtained your much coveted Private Pilot's Licence.

Flying with the Services

I will begin with a brief picture of the flying scene in Britain. It is possible, of course, to train as a pilot with one of the armed forces, but for this you need to be young and medically fit to a high standard, have attained certain educational levels, pass a rigid selection procedure and then agree to serve for a guaranteed number of years. Details differ with each of the three Services, but if you consider yourself to be eligible and you are prepared to operate in a disciplined environment for a considerable time, then do not dismiss the idea. The training offered is thorough and you are paid for doing it. At the end of the agreed term you will have a good background in flying, whether you wish to go into aviation commercially or to continue flying purely for personal pleasure.

There are a few exceptions but, in the main, pilots in the Royal Navy or the Army fly helicopters while the majority of pilots in the Royal Air Force fly fixed-wing machines. All receive basic training on fixed-wing aeroplanes. In the R.A.F. there is a variety of options. It is possible to become an instructor on light single piston-engined trainers, or a fighter pilot, to be on heavy transport duties or on long-range maritime patrol work. Although I have spent nearly all my working life in the world of light civil aviation, I am grateful that I was fortunate enough to train and fly as a Service pilot, for despite the long time lapse, this has given me a solid base on which to build subsequent experience. Not everyone can be as fortunate — and some people do not wish to become involved with military activities. However, if this does appeal, telephone directories and press advertisements will give you the starting points. For younger people in their late teens, the R.A.F. Flying Scholarship and Special Award schemes and, for those a little older, the University Air Squadrons, offer considerable opportunities for learning to fly.

General Aviation

Civil aviation is composed of a number of differing activities that are as far apart as are cruise liners and coracles. The term general aviation (G.A.) is used in many places and covers virtually everything that flies apart from military aircraft and airliners. Within G.A. fall flying training, private flying, crop spraying and dusting, business aviation, charter and taxi work, most helicopters and related activities, such as gliding, hang-gliding, parachuting, ballooning and microlight operations. All these are under the jurisdiction of the Civil Aviation Authority (C.A.A.), which in turn is responsible to the Department of Transport (D.Tp.). We concern ourselves mainly with the first two on the list, beginning with the training aspect.

Firstly, all flying training must be carried out from either a licensed aerodrome or one that is Government owned. The aircraft to be used must be certificated in the transport category and must have a full set of dual controls. The person in charge of training must hold a full Instructor Rating, although tuition under supervision from the ground may be carried out by a holder of an Assistant Instructor Rating.

A licensed aerodrome may be of any stature from a large international aiport to a small rural all-grass airfield. The licence is the common factor and this ensures that certain conditions have been met; for instance, there must be a fire fighting facility (fortunately, very rarely needed with light aircraft) and no fixed obstructions on or near the ends or the sides of the runway, on which you will be taking off and landing. Although you cannot learn to fly at Heathrow or Gatwick, most other airports have private training facilities, as do nearly all G.A. aerodromes. We will discuss this in more detail in Chapter 2.

The aeroplane must meet certain requirements to have a Certificate of Airworthiness (C. of A.) and to be maintained in the Transport Category. It must undergo a servicing schedule, based on both the number of hours flown and on calendar time. There are limitations on the permitted length of the working life of the engine, on instruments and on many component parts. Log book records must be kept to ensure that these requirements are met. Full dual controls must be fitted, enabling either you or your instructor to fly the machine and giving you the opportunity to 'follow through' certain exercises being flown by your mentor.

The person who teaches you to fly must be not only a licensed and experienced pilot, but also he will have undergone a specialised course to qualify as an instructor or assistant instructor. If he is in the assistant category he will have received the full course of training, but he may not be so experienced in the training field as the person with a full rating. The assistant may teach you all the exercises that you need to cover, but as a wise precaution he is required to pass you to a full instructor before you are cleared for your first ever solo flight or your first cross-country trip on your own.

Since January 1987 the C.A.A. has insisted that all training must be carried out to an approved syllabus, so the Authority calls for sufficient legislation to give you a level of protection which contributes towards the very high standard of safety in private flying. Beyond this, however, it is a matter of communication between the student and the instructor. The C.A.A. tells him *what* he must teach you and what sequences you should practise, but not precisely *how* to put it over to you.

Flying schools and clubs

Although a qualified instructor may operate entirely on his own (so long as he complies with the aerodrome, aircraft and training syllabus requirements), this is not the usual practice. Flying schools and flying clubs are spread all over the British Isles. There is no particular difference between a school and a club and sometimes there is little more in the choice than the name, but the former tends to be larger and operated by a commercial company, while the latter may be a more democratically-based concern owned by its members. However, many clubs are operated by companies. There are flying groups, which may be co-ownership organisations or just small flying clubs, usually functioning on a part-time voluntary basis. It is not possible, and certainly not sensible, to try to say that one type of organisation is better than another. Much depends on the people who are running it, and a place that suits one person's outlook and temperament may not be so satisfactory for another. This, though, need not be a cause for worry, for here I am explaining the set-up only and in the next chapter I will give a few cues and clues on how to find the right one.

Aerodromes, aeroplanes and instructors

Considerable freedom remains for the person who wishes to fly purely for personal pleasure. To provide a form of mutual protection, major airports have controlled airspace around them and the main routes used by commercial operators are given the status of airways. As a student or new private pilot you will keep clear of these and other areas of special space, but most of the air over Britain is not controlled and once you have obtained your licence many of the constraints imposed on a trainee are removed. You may fly an aeroplane with a private category C. of A. or even one without a certificate, having instead a permit to fly (which makes the maintenance less expensive) and you may fly in and out of aerodromes that are not licensed — or even to and from private airstrips, many dozens of which exist around the country. Although the C.A.A. takes action against offenders, especially those who endanger the lives of others by penetrating controlled airspace without prior clearance, the scope for a private pilot is extensive, with a variety of available activities to cover the needs, interests and wishes of most people. Despite what many people may say, we have more freedom of flight in Britain than in many other countries.

When you start learning to fly, you will make new friends. You will meet people who will share your queries, problems, occasional frustrations and, most important of all, your enthusiasm for flying and all the pleasures that are associated with it. Apart from the work that you put into learning, you will find a chance for socialising in the unique atmosphere of aviation. Although flying appeals to members of all sections of the community (and some student pilots are known to have given up all luxuries, saving every possible penny and perhaps cycling to the aerodrome for lessons), out of a population of approximately 54 million people, only about 15,000 — or one in 3,500 — hold Private Pilots' Licences. Perhaps there is an attraction and a challenge in becoming an addition to that small band.

2
Getting Started

Choosing where to learn

Depending on where you live, you may or may not have a large choice of places at which you are able to fly. Not surprisingly, with most of the population in the south-east, flying training organisations are spread most thickly in the area surrounding London, but other parts of the country offer several options. There may be only one aerodrome within easy reach of your home, but there could be several schools or clubs based there and this offers certain advantages, enabling you to choose your centre without spending hours travelling round from one to another, in search of your chosen place.

Although you may have your first flying lesson anywhere and you are not compelled to continue your course at the same establishment, both time and effort spent in finding the right centre from the start may prove advantageous. The atmosphere, knowing the people and the familiarity with the surroundings help to make you feel at ease and this is important when you wish to devote your attention — and your money — directly to the task of flying and all that goes with it. Let's consider a few of the variables to be found at schools and clubs.

Airport or aerodrome
A small aerodrome may be operated by the organisation that runs the flying training organisation, in which case you will not have the problem of being just one small part of the overall flying activity there. At the other extreme a flying club may be tucked away in an obscure corner of a major airport, where pilots of light training aircraft may be treated as 'second class citizens' and continually 'held' (delayed) while the bigger revenue-earning machines receive all the priority treatment. However, the dividing line is not usually as clear-cut as that, for attitude of mind plays a far larger part than does the amount of traffic. There are very few really

busy airports today and often those that welcome light aircraft handle considerably more intensive traffic than others that discourage club and private machines. With the right will, it is possible for all types of aviation activity to be slotted in happily, with the minimum of delay or frustration for everyone. So, if you have a choice of aerodrome at which to learn, you will be wise to enquire about this at each place — and to observe activities yourself.

Training centres

Even without any aviation knowledge you can assess many qualities of a training centre. Are yesterday's stale coffee cups lying about? Are the instructors and staff presentable? Do you receive positive help and attention when you make enquiries? What are the charges and the bases on which the charges are made? (Do you pay purely by the flying hour, or for a course including ground tuition and equipment; and are there any extras?) Are the space and facilities adequate for working and relaxing? (Time spent just 'being around the place', watching and listening, talking to fellow students, observing other people going to, from and flying the aircraft is not time wasted; you can learn from the activities of others.) If you are likely to devote long periods at a time to your training, such as whole days, are meals or at least snacks available? Even if not at the centre, on the aerodrome or very close to it? Does the establishment operate on a full-time basis or is it run by volunteers at weekends? The relevance is not one of standards, for many part-time clubs and groups are run by devoted enthusiasts who put more effort and energy into the training task than may be the case at some of the larger places. The significance is one of availability, for unless all your flying is to be at weekends, you will need to know whether you can book at almost any time on any day.

If time allows and there are several centres within easy reach, look at more than one place. You may not be in a position to decide that one is better than another, but most probably you will feel that one suits you more readily. We all have different attitudes and outlooks, so not every person will seek the same type of place. However, think carefully about the purpose of your enrolment with a school or club. Most probably you intend to learn to fly purely for personal pleasure and therefore you will wish to enjoy your time in the air and on the ground. Remember that flying requires concentration and effort on both your part and on the parts of those who are to teach you. You will wish to obtain maximum value in both time and money, so you will not gain if there are too many external distractions. My main point here concerns the working and the social sides of a flying club. Each is important and the bar may be essential to subsidise the operational side, but flying is a serious affair and should be separated, especially during a person's training stages.

Club amenities
I have seen flying instructors doubling as barmen, with the flight record sheet in the lounge amongst the beer glasses. This cannot be good. On the other hand, I have seen flight offices entirely separated from the social amenities or even, in extreme cases, training centres where the management will not permit bars on the premises. Although this puritanical approach may mean a loss of valuable social discourse after flying, it does remove temptation and encourages all concerned to concentrate on what they should be doing. I have been asked by dozens of people to recommend where they should fly and I have tried to be impartial, for nowadays I am not personally connected in any way with a school or club. Interestingly, and quite independently, three acquaintances in the South Midlands sought guidance and I felt that an individual should make his or her own final decision based only on initial advice. I gave the same answers to all three, suggesting that they should look at three named places that were very different from each other. One had an active social element that tended to take priority over the flying, another was small but 'matey' and the third was in the rather formal no-bar category. All three enquirers

inspected the three centres and all chose the same place: the third, which also would have been my first choice. One said afterwards that it was a 'bit clinical', but it provided just what he wanted in the form of a serious course of training for the Private Pilot's Licence. The other two came back to me long afterwards and said that they had no regrets, as the sound tuition had provided a solid base on which to build their subsequent — and less supervised — flying experience. In fairness to all, though, perhaps I should add that these three people were mature and busy adults who were not seeking new social outlets: they wanted to learn to fly quickly and well.

If you go to a place with a strong 'club' atmosphere, let me stress that in itself this is not necessarily a bad move. Some people operate more effectively if left alone to do their own thinking and learning, while others benefit more from social chat. To talk flying in the evening over a glass or two can be beneficial and relaxing, but to be in a bar atmosphere during the working day is not to be encouraged. Certainly you must not drink anything alcoholic before flying and the further apart the social and flying sides are kept, the better.

When you have found somewhere that seems to suit you find out more about it. A leaflet giving brief details of the facilities, the course and the costs should be available. However, before delving too deeply into the longer-term factors, you may wish to discover what flying in a light aeroplane is all about. Perhaps you have been aboard airliners on scheduled services or on inclusive-tour holidays, but there is little similarity between that and the personal atmosphere of private flying in a light aeroplane. In the latter, the machine is in the air just for you. It is not under rigid control of an air traffic control system when you are clear of the aerodrome and it goes up, down, to the left or to the right just as you or your instructor may choose. That is the freedom of flight and one of its many attractions. Despite control zones, airways and other areas that exist mainly for the 'heavy brigade', most of the airspace is available for you and your fellow fliers to use as you wish.

A trial lesson

The first positive move is to book a trial lesson. This is a strange term, for who is on trial and for what? Certainly it is not you who are being judged, for the aim is for you to experience the sensation of flight and for you to decide whether you like it. Generally, one such trip is sufficient for a person to reach a verdict. Most individuals enjoy it very much and many wish there and then to enrol for a full course to obtain a licence. However, if you are not wholly happy on the first time, there may be some underlying reason which is only temporary. For instance you may be a little 'off' that day, or the weather conditions may be somewhat rougher than usual, so be careful not to throw away the idea too hastily. I failed to enjoy either of my first two flights, but the 'bug bit' on my third time in the air and never, never have I regretted devoting most of my life to aviation.

You may be able to have your first flight without booking in advance or you may need to reserve a date and time ahead. You need no special equipment and in a modern aeroplane you will not need to wear heavy overalls or boots. Normal everyday clothes will suffice, but you may be happier if you dress casually, for comfort is essential for success in the air. I dislike having a tie round my neck when I fly, so I remove or at least loosen it and open the top shirt button before getting into an aeroplane; I recommend this to others.

There are several types of aircraft in use at flying schools and clubs, but nearly all are monoplanes with enclosed cabins and side-by-side seating. At this stage the type is not particularly important, for whatever is used will have full dual controls, so that either you or the instructor can fly it. However, among the more widely-used types are the Cessna 152 and the Piper Tomahawk, both of United States origin; also there are several French aircraft in the Robin series and a British machine, the Slingsby Firefly.

On your trial lesson you will meet your instructor, who will ask you a few straightforward questions. Have you flown before? If so, what in and how many times? Have you handled the controls? It may be easier if you have done none of these things, for then both you and your mentor are starting at the beginning, but if you have a little previous experience it is important for you to say so. This will help both of you. Your guide will check the weather, enter the proposed flight on the record sheet and complete any other formalities that may be needed. At some aerodromes he may need to ring air traffic control to book a movement slot, although in most cases this is unnecessary and a call on the aircraft's radio will suffice.

When you have walked to the aeroplane, the instructor will look round it on a pre-flight inspection to ensure that no damage has occurred since the previous flight or since it has been checked by the engineers (a flying stone could have 'nicked' the propeller or something sharp could be embedded in a tyre). Self-discipline is essential with flying and we must not omit any checks or procedures. At this stage you will not need to concern yourself with the details of this external check, but take a quiet look at the machine to see if it is sensibly clean inside and out; this could tell you quite a lot!

You will be guided into the cockpit. The method of entry will depend on whether the wing is set high or low, but take note of the advice given to you as you may tread only in certain places. Once aboard, comfort comes again to the fore, so the seat position should be correct and, if applicable, the pedals should be adjusted. As in a car, you *must* wear the safety harness and this should fit tightly. You may be given a headset so that you can hear the spoken word without too much intrusion from other noises and this also should be comfortable.

The instructor will carry out certain simple checks before he starts the engine. Purely for your interest he may tell you what he is doing, but you are not expected to absorb any great detail. This is intended as a flight for you to enjoy. You are not on test; you are putting flying on test, to see if it appeals and the chances are that it will. Relax, for you are in the capable care of a qualified flying instructor who will know what is sensible for you to be asked to do and what is best left entirely to him. He will carry out some checks in the cockpit, call on the radio for clearance to taxi out and move slowly towards the appropriate runway. Do not worry if you cannot understand what is being said on the radio. This is simply a matter of practice and experience and it will all become clear quite quickly.

The procedure for a trial lesson is left largely to the instructor. He may, or may not, point out much detail during the take-off, while he may ask you to rest your hands and feet on the controls early in the flight. He will do the work, of course, but you will gain an early appreciation of the small amount of movement that is needed to obtain any results. He will suggest various things to look at, both outside to give you an idea of scale as height increases, and inside for you to get an impression of what is happening. He may show you the speed, or the height, but when well clear of the aerodrome he will give you the chance to see and feel what flying is all about and how an aeroplane responds to your handling. Before you can make the machine do what you want, you need to understand the effects of the controls and this will be when you discover that only small pressures are needed to make the aeroplane change its attitude. Everything is logical: easing the control column forwards lowers the nose; easing it back raises the nose. Later you will notice that, as with a car going downhill, lowering the nose causes the speed to increase and, of course, vice versa. Interestingly, an aeroplane flies itself more smoothly than the average pilot flies it, so take comfort when your guide takes his hands off the column and you will see that the machine just goes on as before. There is no struggle with the controls to keep an aeroplane flying!

Your first flight will be short. On the way back, various local landmarks will be pointed out to you and you will be surprised how neatly laid-out everywhere seems and how small a familiar church, railway station, country house, or town hall appears from above. Soon you will be back in the aerodrome circuit and getting confused again by the radio calls, but, as before, they are not your concern yet. Even the aerodrome may look too small to land on, but, for the person beside you, there is more than enough space. A series of gentle turns round the airfield, an approach, a smooth uneventful landing and the flight is over. Whilst taxying back to the parking area, you and the instructor may discuss a few points, but remember that the next move is yours. It is you who wish to learn to fly, so you must make the decision. Do not just pay and go away. Think about the pleasures that can lie ahead and, if you have enjoyed your first experience in the pilot's seat, make the necessary arrangements for further flights on a course towards obtaining a P.P.L.

The P.P.L. course

There are very few people who are incapable of learning to fly, even though some take longer than others, so have no fear about your ability to master what may seem to be a complex process. The course for the Private Pilot's Licence is geared to take you steadily through various exercises and sequences. There are some marvellous experiences in prospect, such as your first ever solo flight, your first cross-country trip, the first time that you land away at another aerodrome and, of course, the licence itself. Then there are many more pleasures to follow.

Cost
Naturally I hope that you will elect to go ahead, but there are a few points to consider before you do so. An important point is cost; can you afford the course? At first you may think not, but perhaps there are other pleasures that you can forgo to reduce your regular outgoings. Then there is the possibility of payment on a credit scheme; several flying schools and clubs offer a deferred-payment system through a recognised finance company. If you are keen, you will find a way of beating the monetary obstacle, so look at all possibilities.

Health
A second point to consider is your health. A private pilot does not need to be exceptionally fit or strong, but there are a few basic requirements, mainly in relation to heart, eyes and ears. Spectacles, though, are not in themselves a bar and that may be good news for you. Before you may fly solo — that is,

on your own — you must hold a valid medical certificate, for which you need to have a straightforward examination by a doctor approved by the Civil Aviation Authority. The flying centre will give you the name and address of a local doctor.

Most people pass this easily, but just in case you have some condition that may prevent you from obtaining a pilot's licence, there is little point in spending much money on a pastime that leads to nothing. A more important point, though, is the possibility that you will forget to have the examination and the time may come for you to fly on your own — that coveted first solo — and your instructor will not be allowed to let you go. What a frustrating thought. So put that right before it happens. Some useful guidelines about medical standards and health generally appear in Appendix 1.

Time

The final matter to consider is your availability, for to make a success of the course and not to waste money, you need to have some continuity throughout your training, not just for each flight, but with time to think, study and attend ground tuition. Do not shirk this, for it is as important as the time spent in the air.

In case you wonder how much time you should devote to your new pastime, try this for guidance. You should aim to fly at least once a week, for occasionally you will miss a lesson due to bad weather and then there will be a fortnight's gap. Then, if you can, you will gain by trying to fit in a flight to compensate for the one you have lost. Continuity really is important, for after a long gap you will spend the first fifteen minutes or so of the next lesson re-tracing the threads from the previous session. This wastes time and money.

One possibility is to have a holiday from work for a week or so and attend on a full-time basis to cover a worthwhile section of the course. The best move would be to have three or four lessons beforehand on a part-time basis. However, your powers of concentration will wane if you try to do too much in too short a time. You will be wise to have not more than two lessons each day, with a gap of three or four hours between, during which you can use the time on the ground to study and watch other people in and around aeroplanes. Before fixing your week off, check with the training centre that there will be sufficient spare capacity then for you to receive the devoted time and attention that you will expect. Also, consider the time of year in relation to both the weather and the hours of daylight, for during most of your early flying you will need good visibility and clear natural horizons.

Making your decision
Take another look at the centre and satisfy yourself that it seems to be the right place for you. Look and listen. Are other students receiving the attention they need? Are they having their lessons at approximately the time for which they have booked? Do there appear to be adequate facilities for the ground tuition that you will require (such as evening lectures, pre- and post-flight briefings and training notes) or are you left to sort all this for yourself in whatever way you can?

Finally, you may be baffled by hearing or seeing that the course for the Private Pilot's Licence is approved by the Civil Aviation Authority. This does not mean that the place is necessarily better than the club next door which may not hold such approval. The C.A.A.'s approval is based on certain fixed criteria, calling for a full-time chief flying instructor with a specific licence, certain items of equipment, records, accommodation and so on, but the system has not proved to be wholly successful and it is being discarded. It may be replaced by a scheme calling for *all* flying training organisations to be registered with the Authority and then a centre will be required to display a certificate to this effect. When this comes into force, all training for a licence, or an added rating on that licence, must be carried out at a recognised centre. The only exception is a family clause whereby, for example, a father (so long as he is a qualified flying instructor) may teach his son to fly on a private basis. In the meantime, though, a requirement has been introduced calling for all training to be conducted to a syllabus that has been approved by the C.A.A. This interim measure came into effect on 1 January 1987.

3
The Path to your First Solo

Preparation for the course

You are about to enrol on a course for the Private Pilot's Licence. Most probably you will be asked to join a club or register with a school. Read the wording before signing any membership form! In general, the forms are straightforward and there are no catches, but there are a few points, such as your liabilities, which you should check. Also, if not explained on the form, ask about insurance. Almost certainly there will be no form of protection for you personally. Although private flying is about the safest of all the pastimes that involve any additional risks to those of everyday life, you may be wise to enquire whether any form of personal accident/injury cover is on offer. If not, you have no cause for dismay, for several schemes are available and the most commonly used plan is organised on a national basis through the Aircraft Owners' and Pilots' Association of the U.K. (see p. 126). Ensure that any cover already in force will not be invalidated if you fly; fortunately many insurance companies are opening their minds and are learning not to treat flying as something that is yet to come, but a few remain rigid. If you are asked for a substantial additional sum it is worth considering changing your broker. All this may be a nuisance, but flying will take much of your time and an hour or so spent getting this right before you start can avoid unlikely, but possible, anguish later.

Find out exactly what you will obtain for your money. There is no standard costing pattern among the pilot training organisations and clearly, as with the market place generally, some will give you better value than others. There are several possibilities, such as an enrolment fee, an hourly flying rate (possibly a little higher for dual than for solo time), with additional charges for your logbook, maps, training publications and so on; an inclusive fee embracing a course of a given number of hours and all ancillary expenses, with an extra charge only for any additional flying time that you may need; or a training rate, with each hourly charge covering all the additional trimmings, which applies for all flying until you gain your licence.

No particular scheme is necessarily better than another, but do take care to check what you will be getting and for how much. Most probably desirable extras, such as evening lectures, will be charged separately, but the cost will be minimal compared with the flying charges and I cannot stress too strongly the importance of taking any ground tuition that may be available. There is more to flying than just flying!

If you are fortunate enough to be able to pay for all or part of the course in advance, then make sure that you are offered a discount for letting the club have your money in their bank before they have given you a service and that, if you discontinue the course for any reason, a realistic refund will be made without argument or unreasonable delay. On two occasions I have been asked to act as the go-between in a situation created by a dissatisfied customer who wanted his money back and the flying centre that refused to pay. In one case the small print said that a course was a contract in which no refund was payable except in the case of a failure on medical grounds — which clearly the aggrieved person had not read; and in the other there was no written agreement. Only the second case was cleared satisfactorily. So take care to check the details before you pay.

Problems which may arise

Running a school or club is not an easy occupation but the majority of training establishments are soundly administered. The problems associated with the British weather may be an inconvenience to you, but to the operator they are multiplied by as many times as the number of students on strength. The elements not only create havoc with a day's well-laid plans, but can cause bottlenecks in the total training programme and serious loss of incoming cash-flow in a business that operates to tight margins. Regular, fixed working hours are impossible for the instructors and staff, with some days of frustration and others of overwork. A successful training operation is possible only if both sides understand each other's difficulties. I will explain a few likely examples.

You may have a booking for midday. The training centre have asked you to arrive early, firstly to give you time to relax and tune your mind to what you will be doing and, secondly, to enable your instructor to give you some pre-flight briefing before the air lesson. You rush through a job to be away from your place of work punctually and refuse to speak to someone who tries to catch you just as you are leaving the premises. Despite these minor problems, you arrive at the aerodrome forty minutes before you are due to fly, only to find that your instructor is not there. You enquire, and discover that he is airborne with another student and he will be thirty minutes late back. This is annoying or, at least, disappointing.

However, usually there is an explanation for such delay. The weather may not have been good enough at the start of the previous person's scheduled starting time, but it improved sufficiently for the lesson to begin half-an-hour later. There have been many arguments about this: should the earlier student forfeit his flight altogether, or have a shortened lesson, or complete the intended exercise and cause a delay to the next comer? Any verdict must be subjective, so turn the tables and think of yourself in the first student's position. Almost certainly you would see an element of fair play in the decision, and you might even be that student on the next occasion!

You are concerned with learning to fly and, as you are paying the training centre to provide you with a course, you may feel that their problems should not be yours. To a point, this is reasonable, but to get the best results you will need a good working relationship with the centre and, especially, with your regular instructor. If there is any hassle, you will be the loser, for your learning ability will be reduced, you will take longer to qualify and, in turn, this will cost you more. Many benefits are to be gained from mutual trust, interest and understanding. If this can be established, the whole process will be much more pleasant.

Relationship between instructor and student

Now to your instructor. An experienced person will be able to assess a student's strengths and weaknesses and will be able to set a pace and pressure to match. Some people need gentle handling, while others respond readily to controlled doses of pressure. A conscientious teacher will be keen to see steady progress by his students and will probably obtain as much personal pleasure from your success as you will. Equally, though, he may be frustrated if you fail to engage your brain. There is no call for very high intelligence or a strong power of absorption, but plain, straightforward common sense heads the list of valuable qualities both now and in your subsequent flying. During the course you will make many mistakes but these are often essential steps to achievement. It is better to err now, under professional guidance, than later when there may be no available help from the next seat! No instructor minds how many mistakes you make, as long as you learn from these and are not guilty of repeating the same error over and over again. This is why time in which to think is important before and after each flight.

When I was a young instructor I learned a very valuable lesson from another who had been in the flying training business for many years. He said that a pound note (then the cost of about twenty minutes flying!) was the most effective tool of persuasion that he had met. If someone was being slow to learn and insisted on making the same mistakes over and over again, he would hold the note conspicuously in his hand and nearly throw it overboard. This attracted the student's attention, sometimes leading to the question 'Why are you doing that?' Nearly always the reply, such as 'You have made that same mistake five times in the past twenty minutes and in effect you have just thrown away that amount of money' brought instant response in quicker learning! No doubt a ten pound note would have a similar effect today.

The quickest learner does not necessarily become the best pilot. Often the slow starter, who makes all the mistakes in the book but who learns from them, gains a more thorough

Ground tuition forms an essential part of your course for the Private Pilot's Licence

knowledge. This gives him a firmer foundation on which to build subsequent experience and can be valuable later when flying is less closely supervised. As a student, you can learn far more from studying and rectifying your own mistakes than you can from even the best instructor. Think about that regularly during your course, for a combination of a good teacher and a responsive learner must lead to success.

Throughout your training the pattern of the course will consist of a logical series of lessons based on a set syllabus. The Civil Aviation Authority dictates that to qualify for your Private Pilot's Licence you must fly a minimum of forty hours. There are some guidelines to the breakdown of that time but, in the main, the actual time spent on each exercise will depend on you and your progress. You will learn the effects of the controls, straight and level flight, climbing and descending, level turns, turns on the climb and on the descent and then you will have a basic knowledge of the way to make an aeroplane do more or less what you want it to do in the air. There is more to it than that, of course, but if you can fly the machine level, go up or down and turn onto selected headings, then you have the main idea. You will be inaccurate at first but this improves with practice. Your standards of handling will improve as you go on, but you can set yourself target standards and insist on attaining them. The sooner you can begin to make the most of your time in the air, the more money you will save. The requirement for forty hours is a minimum and no instructor or training establishment can guarantee that you will reach the necessary standard within that time. Largely it must be up to you and I must stress that your effort is as important as that of your instructor.

Excessive concentration can lead to tension. Clearly, you will need to find your own level of cockpit activity and you must endeavour to remain reasonably relaxed. What happens outside the aeroplane, both before and after flight, in terms of briefings from your instructor, your own pre-flight preparation and post flight replay, is not only just as important as your work in the air, but also it is free. After a lesson, think about the exercises that you have carried out, note down any doubts and/or queries and ask your instructor *before* the next flight. This can save time and money through a better understanding of what you are doing and therefore must lead to improved performance.

After several lessons you will get to know your instructor and should feel at ease with him or her. However, an occasional change of tutor is not a bad move, for if you become accustomed to flying with the same person you may feel ill at ease when later you have a strange person beside you. Ideally, two instructors prior to the first solo would be appropriate, but if you find that you have been booked to fly with different individuals on each of several consecutive flights, then you would be wise to register your discontent; not with the instructor, for it is unlikely to be his fault and he may feel affronted (which would be unfortunate if you should fly with him again later), but at management or chief instructor level. In the very rare event of an unworkable combination of instructor and student — caused by a personality clash — normally the instructor will arrange for a change, but if not, then you should put in a quiet request for a new mentor. This does not reflect badly on either party, for in all paths of life there are a few people who cannot relate mutually on a workable basis.

Stalling

You will hear many references to the word 'stalling'. This does not refer to the engine stopping, as it does in a car, but is a term relating to the flow of air over and beneath the wings of an aeroplane. Normally, this flows smoothly and freely, generating the lift that enables the machine to fly, but if the angle of the wing becomes steeper than usual to the oncoming airflow, such as having the nose too high and/or the speed too low, the air breaks away from its smooth path and forms eddies. You cannot see this, but you may have witnessed similar disturbances in rivers when obstructions disturb the normal movement of the water. When this break-away occurs, known as the stall, the wing loses some of its lift and it is necessary to reduce the angle at which the oncoming air meets the wing. Until a few years ago this was taught as a wholly detached exercise and it seemed to have little practical relevance to the average student. However, a recent improvement in training technique has been the introduction of slow speed flight, in which you will have the opportunity to experience and recognise the changing flight conditions which lead to the normal type of stall.

I am not giving you a lesson in theory of flight, but your air exercises will be more beneficial and easier to understand if you have some idea of why things happen. Feel plays a part in flying, for if you fly at a low speed, the air passes the wings more slowly, so there is less resistance to movement of the controls and you need to move them more generously to obtain the required results. Conversely, at high speed, the controls are tighter in feel and need only minimal movement. Therefore, if you become accustomed to a usual level of both feel and response, you will notice the difference if you fly more slowly (or much faster) than usual. The idea behind the new slow-speed exercise is to give you experience in both recognising and dealing with an unusual flight condition, so that you will rectify the situation *before* the angle and/or speed lead you to the stall itself. You will learn the stall and the recovery — a very straightforward operation — but the primary purpose will be to teach you stall avoidance. This is one of the most important points that you will learn and will be of permanent value in your later flying.

Examinations

So far I have referred almost entirely to the flying side but there are some supporting ground subjects which must be studied alongside your tuition in the aeroplane. You will need to take very straightforward multiple-choice examinations in Aviation Law, Flight Rules and Procedures and, a little later, in both Navigation and in Meteorology. The C.A.A.'s Civil Air Publication (C.A.P.) 53 explains the extent of the syllabus and a copy of this will be available at your flying centre, but make certain to devote sufficient time and thought to this rather than doing some eleventh-hour cramming. There are many good books and your instructor will advise you, but you should attach yourself to whatever ground instructional facilities are available. Evening lectures are provided at most places and these offer ideal opportunities for subject concentration, with you and your fellow students learning collectively in an ideal environment. You must not overlook the importance of this side of your training. The C.A.A. allows twelve months between passing the ground examinations and completing the application for your pilot's licence.

I have mentioned the importance of your ground studies and now you will reach the stage at which you will need to prove your knowledge. Since 1 January 1987, the C.A.A. has introduced a requirement for the written examination in Aviation Law, Flight Rules and Procedures to be passed before the first solo flight.

From the start you should spend sufficient time in studying all the related ground subjects. You do not require a high standard of academic ability, but to succeed you must take the trouble to learn how an aeroplane flies, the checks and procedures relating to the type of aeroplane in which you are training and the relevant rules of the air. Weather will play a regular role during your course and in your subsequent flying, so take a practical interest in its behaviour patterns. There are several ways in which you can absorb the necessary knowledge, but a most important attribute is to cultivate an active and enquiring interest in what goes on at the aerodrome. Learn not only from what you are doing, but from watching others.

Trimming

Throughout your course you will meet the word 'trim'. This applies to the use of a small lever or wheel in the cockpit which enables you to set the aeroplane for hands-off flight. Each time you alter the speed, the engine power or the attitude of the aircraft — and all these are inter-related — the fore-and-aft load on the control column will vary. On most light types these loads are small, but when an item within easy reach of your hand can remove them entirely, make the most of it. Always remember that after any adjustment to a flight condition, the trim will change, so it must be the last action to take. Proper trimming makes flying much easier and if the aeroplane is set to carry on unaided you are far less likely to lose or gain height, whichever is relevant. Also, you can concentrate on the things that you must do.

You will be taught the correct sequence for each move in any changes of flight condition. For example, to go from level flight to the climb you will first open the throttle, then raise the nose, wait for the speed to settle at its new value, check and adjust the nose attitude if necessary and, finally, trim. This is not just something to learn in parrot style to keep your instructor happy. Think *why* it is the correct procedure and why no other sequence would work. Take time over it.

The circuit

Soon you will come to work on the circuit. This is a most valuable series of exercises, for although its main purpose is to give you practice in the art of taking off, approaching and landing, the supporting procedure provides further experience in many of the lessons already learned: straight and level flight, climbing and descending, level, climbing and descending turns, and use of the trimmer.

In-flight aspects that will be less familiar are the need for judgement and use of the flaps. The last two go together in a neat package and here you must appreciate that the wind has no effect on an aeroplane's movement through the air

Usually a flying school fleet is standardised and here the main type on the flight line is the Cessna 152

(except, if conditions are turbulent, to create bumps), but that it affects everything in relation to its passage over the ground. We will consider first a circuit in calm conditions and then one in a steady wind of, say, twenty knots. Before comparing the two, though, I will give a brief explanation of what a circuit is intended to be.

After taking off we climb to a height of, perhaps, 500 feet and carry out a gentle climbing turn through about ninety degrees, then climb on the new crosswind heading to say, 800 feet. Then we go into level flight before another 90° turn in the same direction, finishing parallel but in the opposite direction to the line of take-off. When we have passed the end of the runway, we turn again through a right angle to put ourselves on the second crosswind or base leg. We reduce power for the descent and when nearly in line with the runway we carry out a descending turn to line-up for a straight approach towards our intended point of touchdown. We use the flaps as required to steepen our approach and to arrive at ground level at the start of the runway.

When there is no wind, the circuit will be relatively easy. If we fly reasonably accurately, after take-off we will continue straight ahead at the aeroplane's normal angle of climb and the runway (or take-off path if there is no runway) will remain directly behind us. At the correct height we start the climbing turn and look over our shoulder to see when we are at right angles to the runway before straightening from the turn. With no wind, the aircraft's heading through the air will be identical with its path over the ground. Our speed through the air and our speed over the ground will be similar. After levelling out and turning parallel to the runway (and throughout this circuit), the airspeed and the ground-speed will remain the same as there is no wind to affect the latter. When we turn onto the base leg, again our angle judgement is unlikely to go adrift, as there is nothing to deflect us from the direction in which we point the aeroplane. Our first error may be that we lower the flaps too late, because on the final approach to the runway for landing there is no wind against us to reduce our ground speed and to increase our angle of descent in relation to the ground.

The second circuit will be less straightforward, but we will assume that we are taking off into the wind. When we line-up to start the turn, in effect we are doing 20 knots through the air before we move (air coming at us or the aeroplane going at the air is identical), so if the machine 'unsticks' from the ground at, say, 40 knots, we need to accelerate through only another 20 knots before we are in the air. This shortens our take-off run, so we start our climb further back than before. Climbing at, say, 60 knots into the wind of 20 knots means that we are covering the ground at only 40 knots, but still ascending at the same rate as before. When we reach the height for our climbing turn we are much closer to the end of the runway than we were on our windless circuit.

This turn will be through fewer than ninety degrees for if we are to track over the ground at right angles to the runway, we need to head the aeroplane in towards the wind. If we fail to do this (and it is a very common omission among students) we will drift in the direction of the wind and when we carry out our second, level turn we may be downwind of the end of the runway. This physically shortens the down-wind leg and as we will travel over the ground at the additional 20 knots of the wind strength, we will have relatively little time in which to complete our checks, assess the position for our third turn and generally we will be rushed. This is among the surest ways to make a mess of our approach and landing. The third turn is even more impor-tant, for here we will need to turn through more than a right angle and if we fail to turn sufficiently on the base leg, we will drift further and further from our planned touchdown point. This will affect our plans for reducing power and for lowering flaps. Accurate judgement leading to correct circuit shape is extremely important.

There are a few other circuit-related points that may be helpful. Whilst usually the pattern is flown left-handed, a few aerodromes operate the other way for particular pur-poses such as avoiding conflicting circuits with other airfields or to avoid over-flying sensitive areas such as hos-pitals. There are other parochial differences, again usually

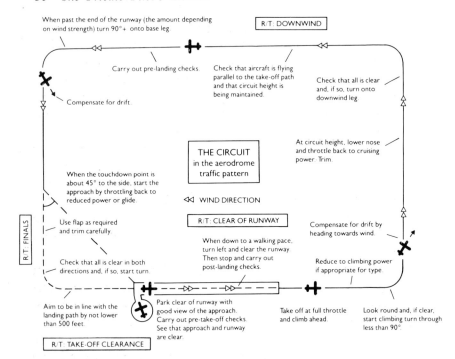

The circuit

for good reasons. Whilst 800 feet is the most commonly practised circuit height, this does not apply everywhere, but the principles are unaffected. See the diagram above.

If you are awaiting a session on the circuit and have time available, see what other students are doing. Are they tending to make repeatedly high approaches and needing to go round again to make several attempts at landing? If so, why? This should tell you that the wind may be unusually light. Check the windsock not just for direction but for strength, too.

What to do if engine fails on take-off

After several sessions on the circuit, with occasional breaks into the local flying area to refresh on low-speed handling and stall avoidance, or just to smoothen any rough edges that need clearing in the comparative peace away from the pressures of the aerodrome traffic zone, you will be almost ready to do a solo flight. Before this, however, you will be shown a safety exercise that you are most unlikely ever to put into practice, but which you must be capable of handling: what to do if the engine should fail shortly after take-off. Modern aero engines are very reliable and serious technical problems are rare, but so far no one has designed anything mechanical that is physically incapable of failing. If the noise stops and you are surrounded by new-found silence, the procedure is to lower the nose to retain that all-important airspeed and then to land as nearly as possible directly ahead , making only essential deviations to avoid hard obstructions. There is a strong inclination to turn round and head back to the aerodrome, but this can be very dangerous and must be avoided. Even if the ground in front of you is not your first choice in ideal landing places, your touch-down speed is low and you are strapped in. With an impact speed that is very much lower than that of the average car accident, you are much safer than you are on the roads. The chances of being personally unharmed are strongly in your favour. Anyhow, you are very unlikely even to need to put it to the test. It is just a part of the 'belt and braces' policy that contributes to the high standards of safety that apply to the world of private flying.

First Solo Flight

Some people worry about the time taken to reach the first solo. There is a tendency to compare the number of hours needed by one student with those of another who may make the grade in half the time. Some are impatient and even cause delay to the great day because they are concentrating more on what is to come than on what they should be doing. Others find the occasion comes upon them when least expected. Many factors come into play and my only advice is to get on with the task of learning to fly. Your instructor will decide to let you go alone when his experience tells him that you are ready. Only he can assess this. There is no way in which worrying will hasten the event, but it could cause delay.

The anticipation before a first solo flight can be very exciting, but it does not compare with the retrospective sense of achievement — when you have completed a circuit alone and taxyed back to the parking spot on the flight line. Whether you retire to the bar to celebrate or just re-live the experience alone in the strength of your own imagination, remember that this is a unique occasion in your life and never, never can it be repeated.

You have flown alone. You never will regret or forget it. This is the first major step towards the freedom of flight that is ahead of you.

4
On to that Coveted Pilot's Licence

After completing your first solo flight successfully you have just passed a milestone and you may feel that the next session of dual with an instructor is an anti-climax. If you have flown safely and satisfactorily on your own, why should the instructor need to accompany you before you are let loose again?

When you flew solo for the first time, the required conditions would be in your favour: the wind was not too strong, it was not gusting or blowing too severely *across* the runway, the visibility was reasonable, you were 'on form' and there was not too much competing traffic in the circuit. On your next visit all these variables could have changed. The wind might be stronger, or lighter (perhaps causing you to overshoot the planned point of touchdown), it could be in the form of a crosswind from the opposite side to that to which you have been accustomed, a different runway (or the same one from the opposite end) might be in use, or you may be temporarily 'off tune' with flying. Your instructor will come with you for a few circuits and then, if all is well, he may send you off to do, say, three on your own. A similar, but probably shorter, check flight will precede your third solo, but the pattern must depend on several factors, not the least of which is the length of the time gap between your flights. You are at a stage where regular attendance and continuity are important.

Sometimes from now you will visit the aerodrome and hope to carry out some solo flying. Occasionally, you will arrive to be told that conditions are not suitable. You will have either a dual lesson on some more advanced exercises, or there will be no flying at all. Of course you will be disappointed, but take care not to allow yourself to be too frustrated. The disinterested student takes this as a cue to turn round and go home or back to the office. Avoid being guilty of that. You have much to learn and if you have organised your day to include a couple of hours or so at the centre, use that time to full advantage. Find out what you will be doing next and read about it, brush up your checks and procedures, or try to improve your radio-telephony technique. Soon you will be getting away from the home aerodrome and starting on cross-country navigation, so look to see what the routes will be. Practise drawing track lines on a topographical map, then calculate the headings that you will need to set with certain wind strengths and directions. You are taught how to do these things, but this is no substitute for practice and experience.

You will be alternating between dual and solo sequences. With your instructor you will be refreshed on slow-speed handling leading to the stall and recovery. You will learn to practise forced landings with and without power. The first gives you an insight into the procedure for an unscheduled landing away from home, if you should be caught in bad weather, and the second is the procedure to follow in the very unlikely event of an engine failure. Remember, an aeroplane remains just as controllable without an engine as with one, (after all, a glider operates on similar principles and even starts without one!), so you will learn and practise a proven procedure for gliding down into a field.

Other exercises will include lessons in steeper turns than those to which you are accustomed and operation at minimum level. The latter is not an invitation to make yourself a nuisance just flying low for the sake of it, but to enable you to experience the visual effect of the wind, especially on turns in various directions, so that you will rely on your airspeed indicator and not on false impressions. For example, consider flying at an airspeed of 80 knots into a wind of 20 knots and turning through 180 degrees downwind. On the first stage, your speed over the ground would be 60 knots and on the second stage 100 knots. You must avoid the temptation of thinking that you are *really* going faster (i.e., through the air) and you must resist the tendency to raise the nose or throttle back, either (and certainly both) of which could lead to a stall. Also, this exercise illustrates the false visual effects of turns in relation to wind direction, i.e. appearing to be blown out of or into the turns. Therefore, it is useful in helping you to understand the differences between airspeeds and groundspeeds, and in making you a better and safer pilot. Apart from flying by reference to instruments, it is the only lesson in the syllabus that you will not carry out on your own.

At this stage you should be gaining maximum enjoyment from your flying, as you learn new skills with your instructor and practise skills already learned on your own. Solo flying is particularly pleasant when the weather, the wind and other factors are in your favour, but remember to use it to advantage. Set yourself steadily increasing levels of accuracy, as soon you will be starting on navigation and here sloppy flying will play havoc with your calculations — and therefore your results. Most people enjoy challenges, and here is just such an opportunity. If your aim is to fly at 80 knots at 2500 feet, do so; not at 73 knots climbing slowly to 3000 feet! (Think again about our old friend the trimmer.)

If you would like to experience flying at its very best, book one of your flights, preferably a solo one, as near to the end of the day as possible. This will give you a taste of the brand of flying that holds an irresistible appeal to many pilots. Usually, in the hour or so before dusk, the wind is light, the air is smooth, the shadows are long and you will find that your handling is much more accurate. Take care, though, not to gain all your experience in these ideal conditions, for you need practice in moderate winds and when there are a few bumps in the air. Also, of course, there is little sense in starting on cross-country flights when daylight is running out. Pre-dusk circuits are hard to beat for the sheer simple pleasure of flying for its own sake.

Navigation

There are many reasons for wanting to learn to fly although, surprisingly, many people cannot explain why they wish to do so. Whatever your ultimate aim you must learn to progress from one place to another with a reasonable level of accuracy. Before starting, you will need some knowledge of the principles of pilot navigation, which includes an understanding of the way in which the wind affects an aeroplane's passage over the ground but not its path through the air. Think back to the circuit and the related diagram, in which we would head the machine in towards the direction from which the wind is blowing in order to achieve the desired track over the ground. This is why, as I mentioned earlier, reasonably accurate flying is essential if our navigation is to work successfully. If we calculate (using a very simple navigation computer) a heading and speed over the ground for a particular height and airspeed and we fail to maintain either or both values, then we will go wrong. If we fly too fast or too slowly, then our planned headings and our timings will be incorrect and if we fly higher or lower than we intended, the wind may differ from that upon which we based our figures. The points I wish to stress here are the importance of allowing plenty of time before a navigation exercise to prepare and plan the flight and, once under way, to fly as accurately as possible. This is when you will discover whether you have used your earlier flying time to full advantage by setting yourself good standards of precision. Your instructor can tell you what to do, but only you can achieve it.

You may hear other pilots talking about radio navigation aids, possibly insisting that with the equipment now available in many light aircraft, map-reading is old fashioned. Don't listen! Many private pilots use very high frequency Omni Range (V.O.R.) as their main artificial aid, but it is *essential* to learn the basic principles of travelling from A to B without such aids. This entails having a known track, setting a heading to achieve it, flying accurately and pin-pointing your position by reference to the map. This is a requirement for the P.P.L. course and it gives a good base upon which later you can build other methods. Occasionally, an aid that depends on an electrical power supply may fail without warning, and you will have to rely on your eyes and your map reading ability. Be prepared and be confident enough to fly cross-country using the traditional way that has worked well since the earliest days of flying.

Your first experience of navigation will be turning onto and maintaining various headings that your instructor calls to you. This will be an appropriate time to remember the need for accuracy in your handling. Do not forget other important aspects, such as height and speed. You may roll out of a turn on to the precise heading that you sought, but if you lose 500 feet and gain 15 knots in the process and this was the start of the first 'leg' of a real cross-country, you could have self-made problems ahead. Another factor to consider is the spot from which you start. If the aim is to set your heading over the centre of the aerodrome (which is the point from which you will have drawn a track line on your map), then try to be over the middle. If you start half a mile to one side, you will be half a mile off your intended track all the way, assuming you fly accurately! If not, it could be more. All this comes back to the importance of not being rushed. Starting the flight accurately is almost as important as the preparation on the ground that preceded it. In short, the more time you allow up to the start of that first leg, the easier, the more successful and the more enjoyable the flight itself will be.

Your first cross-country flight

Your first real cross-country is likely to be a three-legged affair starting and finishing at the home aerodrome. It will be quite short, so will not take you far, but it will give you valuable experience in flying in three main directions and will provide an insight into the effects of wind on ground speeds and required headings. You will be surprised how readily landmarks appear where and when you expect them to appear and almost certainly you will enjoy this new aspect of flying. Previously, you will have concentrated on making the aeroplane do what you intend it to do, but now you have entered a fresh phase in taking it where you want it to go. You are becoming its master.

Solo cross-country

Soon you will have another very special experience: your first solo cross-country flight. Before tackling this you should be ready to take the written examinations in Navigation and

Metereology. For a solo cross-country the weather must be good, especially in terms of visibility (with a good natural horizon) and the height of the cloud base. Again, arrive early: prepare your flight log, check it and hand it to your instructor to examine. He must authorise the flight (indeed, all solo exercises by students must be authorised in writing) and he carries a strong responsibility for its success, so he will not clear you to go until he is satisfied that all is well. Remember the advice and significance of not rushing before a flight. Do everything methodically and you will be surprised how soon you are on the last leg of the route. The sight of the home aerodrome ahead will produce a strong sense of satisfaction and when you are back on the ground

Destination reached! Coventry airport as it might be seen on your first landing-away cross-country flight.

you will reflect happily on the achievement. No words can describe the feelings of contentment, but then flying is unique and only by personal experience can you understand why it has such a strong appeal. This occasion is one that will stay with you for a long time, but take heart, for there are more pleasures over the horizon.

Between your cross-country flights you will continue to receive dual instruction, backed by solo experience, in handling. Mostly these will be repetitions of earlier exercises including various types of turns, low speed flight, stalling, circuits and forced landings, with the aim of refining your level of performance — and increasing your confidence.

Spin recovery procedure
You may hear other pilots talking about spinning, for until 1985 this was a compulsory part of the P.P.L. syllabus, but it has been removed and its need partly replaced by the stall avoidance exercises. A spin occurs if a stall is not corrected, so whilst you are unlikely to meet such an experience in your normal flying activities as a private pilot, you may be offered the opportunity to undergo the spin recovery procedure as an optional extra. If later you intend to learn aerobatics, spinning and recovery will be essential practices so you could gain by starting now. If your aim is touring or taking family or friends round the local area, then there is no necessity for you to do so. However, the more you learn, the more complete a pilot you will be, and if the opportunity arises and the idea appeals rather than appals, take it.

Flying with reference to instruments alone

Another experience that you will meet about now is an introduction to flight by reference to the instruments alone. So far you have kept the aeroplane laterally level by using the natural visual horizon and your level, climbing and descending attitudes have been judged largely by the position of the aircraft's nose in relation to that horizon, with only cross-reference to the dials on the panel. However, it is possible to fly accurately without seeing outside the windows or windscreen. Although you need several hours of tuition and practice in order to do this effectively, a brief insight into the mysteries of instrument flight will show you how to fly out of bad weather immediately you meet it and will convince you not to press-on ahead when you cannot use visual references. These are the reasons for its inclusion in the P.P.L. syllabus, but later as a licensed pilot you will have the chance to take more comprehensive instruction in this if you wish to do so.

Flying tests

Until 1987, there was only one formal flying test ahead of you prior to obtaining your licence. Now, though, a navigation test has been introduced. This is not just a piece of ministerial bureaucracy to make life harder, but is a move based on practical experience of private pilots going adrift and entering forbidden airspace. It is a help to you; for although it has been normal practice for a student to have a dual landing at a strange airfield, previously no instructor was *required* to be with you when you landed away at another aerodrome and you could make several mistakes in the strange environment of someone else's circuit without a guiding hand to put you right. The new test satisfies your instructor, the C.A.A. and you that you can cope away from home without constant supervision, which is precisely what your P.P.L. will entitle you to do. This check flight includes a practice diversion to an unscheduled destination to give you experience in what to do if you meet bad weather on the way to your planned point. It is a very valuable addition to the course.

By now you have learned all the flight exercises that you will need in order to qualify for your pilot's licence, but you should concentrate on improving your standards. You will have one or two flying sessions with an instructor (and at this stage it is beneficial if you have flown with more than one), in order to prepare you for the General Flying Test. At most establishments the Chief Flying Instructor or another experienced person is authorised by the Civil Aviation Authority to conduct the test, so you will be pleased to know that (unlike the case of the driving test) you will not be required to present yourself at a strange place before an unknown examiner. The flight will be carried out in a familiar aeroplane from your home aerodrome, so you will not be expected to face anything that you have not met previously.

The flying test is very straightforward. The person beside you is not there with the aim of failing you. He wants you to qualify just as much as you do, but he has a responsibility to ensure that when he has signed the form for submission to the C.A.A., which issues the licence, you are safe and competent to use the privileges that follow. You will be entitled to fly any relatively light single-engined aeroplane. You will be allowed to fly into any other aerodrome including most busy airports and — perhaps this is the most significant — you will be permitted to take with you passengers who may not have flown before and who will rely solely on you for their peace of mind. Although as a newly fledged pilot you will be wise to continue to seek advice from those able and willing to give it, you will not find help quite so readily available as it has been during your course of training. The instructors are likely to be busy teaching and supervising the students that follow you. So, in a way, the examiner is as much on test as you are, for if he clears you before you are ready and something goes wrong subsequently, he may have some explaining to do!

This check flight is to ensure that you have reached the required standard in all the usual procedures, such as flying straight and level accurately, climbing and descending, turning, low-speed flight leading to the stall and recovery, take-offs, circuits, overshoots (going round again) and landing, and forced landings with and without power. You will be expected to exercise sensible judgment, such as lowering the flaps for landing when they are required and not just at a given height or spot over the ground, or abandoning a landing approach that goes wrong without waiting to be told to do so. Safety and airmanship will play key roles in the process of checking whether you are ready to be let loose on the aviation world. The examiner will note whether you establish and maintain a healthy look-out procedure (where you look is as important as how often), check fuel contents and oil pressure, whether you complete your various cockpit checks (and are not guilty of just saying them), and whether you handle the engine smoothly and use carburettor heat at the right times. Handling the aeroplane accurately is important, but doing so safely and sensibly is even more essential. Therefore, understand the examiner's position if at the end of the flight he says that he would like to run through a few sequences again. He may suggest that you go off alone for half-an-hour or so to practise some specific exercises and then he will fly with you again. This test is your key to flying freedom and you must be ready to receive it.

Apart from the flying check and the straightforward written tests, you will be asked some oral questions about the practical sides of flying. What actions would you take if you go to another aerodrome and require fuel? Is it permissible to fill the seats, the fuel tanks and the luggage space, or would you be loading the aeroplane incorrectly? What is the minimum safe oil pressure and what would you do if you should see it lowering toward this figure? If you approach a strange airport to be told that the runway in use is on a westerly heading and the surface wind is from the north at 22 knots, what would you do?

If you are to receive that coveted licence and be permitted to fly without a close guiding hand, you owe it to yourself, your passengers and to other pilots to know these things and it is right that you should be tested on them. During many years as an examiner of candidates for the P.P.L., frequently I found this verbal question-and-answer session to be more telling than the flight test itself. As I said previously, there is more to flying than just flying, so take care not to cut the corners on the general knowledge and commonsense aspects.

You are ready to apply to the Civil Aviation Authority for your licence. The flying centre will ensure that the necessary examination papers are marked, but check that your personal flying log-book is completed correctly and that you can find your medical certificate. You will need to have flown at least 40 hours, to include a minimum of 10 hours solo. You must have carried out 4 hours of instrument flying tuition and 4 hours of solo cross-country time. However, these are minima, so the chances are that you will have needed more total hours in order to reach the required level of performance.

There will be a fee to pay to the Authority at the time of application. In return you will be issued with a Private Pilot's Licence for aeroplanes in Group A: single-engine machines with total weight not exceeding 12,500 lbs (5,700 kg), enabling you to fly a British registered aircraft anywhere in the world, so long as you do so in weather conditions appropriate to that licence and keep clear of certain restricted airspace.

Soon your new Private Pilot's Licence will arrive in the post. This is another great day in your flying life. Now you may embark on a whole range of new ventures and experiences, with several possible paths to follow, depending on your interests and particular inclinations. In the next few chapters I offer some ideas, but before you embark on anything new let's look at the value of consolidating your present position. You must not waste your latest acquisition!

5
Your New Freedom

Now that you have your new pilot's licence and the privileges that go with it, you may wonder what to do next. Some people have ambitions for further advancement, while others see the P.P.L. as the ultimate target. The flying world has ample space for both, but whatever your eventual intentions, or if so far you have not decided what you want to do, several practical principles based on sound common sense must apply to you as a newly-qualified pilot.

Further help from your flying centre

You have a licence, but to support it you have only the minimum of experience. Most probably you will continue to fly with the centre that has trained you and, for the early stages, you may be wise to do so. Take care not to dismiss the training environment as something that is way behind you, for all pilots should continue to learn throughout their active flying lives. If your are able to continue to obtain some professional help, take advantage of this. A flying club will wish to take care of its aeroplanes and the way of ensuring this is to take care of you. This may mean a requirement for a passenger-carrying check flight before you will be permitted to take anyone with you. This would be followed by a periodical safety check to ensure that you have not developed bad habits. Treat these as bonus facilities, for they can be nothing other than beneficial to both your safety and your general competence as a pilot. At the time of your general flying test for the licence, you were under constant guidance and supervision to enable you to reach the required level of performance. Without someone to criticise, comment and advise, your standard is almost certain to deteriorate and, without being aware, your flying could become dangerous; and that at a time when you may be taking your best friend or loved one for his or her first flight! Therefore, accept help when it is there.

Maintaining skills and standards

The most dangerous pilot of all is the one who becomes excessively confident. If you begin to feel that you are becoming exceptionally good, remember that most people in the skies around you have many times more hours of experience in the air than you have. Be aware of your inexperience and limitations, and fly accordingly. Have respect for your aeroplane, for the weather, for your passengers and for the airspace and its other users. On the other hand, if you tend to be exceptionally cautious and possibly reluctant to go ahead on your own, remember you would not be in possession of a licence unless you had achieved the standard of competence necessary to attain it. Whether you fit into either of these extremes or whether, like most new pilots, you are not at either end of the scale, the paragraphs that follow will be equally relevant. There are certain points which require particular attention.

Loading

If you continue to fly the type of aeroplane on which you have trained and if it is a two-seater you are not likely to meet problems of loading. Unlike a car, in which you may fill all the seats, the petrol tank, all available corners and a roof rack, an aeroplane needs to get into the air and stay there under full control — possibly in bumpy conditions. So there are two aspects to consider. Firstly, the maximum permissible weight at which the machine is cleared to fly and secondly, the way in which the loads are distributed. Whilst your two-seater may be safe with both seats occupied, with tanks filled and, possibly, with the limited luggage space filled, do not assume that you *cannot* overload it. Two heavy occupants and a couple of unusually heavy items of luggage might be too much if full fuel is taken on board. Then the obvious move is not to fill the tanks to capacity, but you must balance the reduced range and endurance that this will create against the distance that you intend to fly. With a larger aeroplane, overloading or incorrect loading is a very distinct possibility and almost certainly you will not be permitted to fill all seats, tanks and spaces. Also if you have trained on a four-seater but have flown only 'two up', the handling characteristics may be quite different when you carry a couple of people behind you. Make sure that you understand the principles of weight and balance. Charts and supporting information will be available for most types of aeroplane you are likely to fly but if not, ask someone in authority and always be cautious.

Limitations
Aeroplanes are designed and officially cleared to do specific things, with clearly laid down limits and limitations. All types that reach regular use are very safe and sound and most are able to accept fairly harsh punishment, but try not to put a machine on trial; you are not a test pilot. There is a speed above which the flaps should not be lowered. Do not use the brakes excessively, or they may fail when you really need them. Carry out only gentle manoeuvres in a loaded machine in bumpy conditions. There is nothing to be gained by flying the aeroplane to its maximum limiting airframe speed (V.N.E.). Remember also that what you do with the aeroplane can affect the engine, which will respond more readily if you treat it correctly. Use smooth throttle movements, keep well within the permitted power settings for prescribed flight conditions, monitor the oil pressure and temperature and remember that even a fully fit engine will let you down if you fail to use the carburettor heat at the right times. If an aeroplane has a certificate of airworthiness in the normal category, aerobatic manoeuvres are forbidden. Even a type with an aerobatic clearance will have limitations, so do not assume that this is a cue to limitless structural strength. It is equally important not to carry out your own personal experiments with manoeuvres which you have not been taught. If you wish to learn aerobatics later, by all means do so, but learn first and live on. I will discuss the subject of aerobatics in Chapter 7.

Weather
Perhaps this is the biggest limiting factor of all, not only to novices but also to very experienced pilots who have learned not to try to beat it. You are flying for your own personal

pleasure, so there is no sense in getting airborne in unsuitable conditions. Another day always awaits you and the pleasure is still ahead. The yardsticks to which you should work are measured not only in relation to your experience, but also in relation to the local terrain. If you are in, for example, East Anglia where the highest object is likely to be a church spire, you may think safely in terms of the cloud base above the height of your departure aerodrome. If you are in parts of Wales, Scotland or the Pennines, however, ground may rise to heights greater than your usual cruising level and clouds packed with solid centres do not allow for a second chance. When mountains or high hills exist near your proposed track you must take special precautions, but if the obstructions are in the vicinity of an aerodrome from which you propose to operate, you should seek advice based on local knowledge. Very localised weather changes occur in some places and these may differ from the conditions expected nationally.

Although British weather is a subject for scorn among many people, it does have much to offer. Very rarely is it extremely hot or extremely cold, while really strong gusty winds occur less frequently than in some parts of the world. Even if you may be unable to go precisely where and when you wish, the majority of days will be suitable for safe and enjoyable flying. If you plan to carry out a cross-country flight and possibly visit another aerodrome for the sheer pleasure of doing so, be flexible. You may have thought about a route to the west, but whilst conditions there may be forecast to deteriorate, possibly all may be well in the opposite direction. So why not go that way? If you do, plan properly first.

Wind

Although we tend to think automatically about visibility, cloud base and the possibility of rain, we should not overlook the overall effects of the direction and strength of the wind. If the wind is strong it may cause just a bumpy flight in the home circuit, but on a cross-country flight with fixed destinations or turning points, the flight will take longer than in no-wind conditions. The wind affects your flight over time and not over distance, so if it is strong you must give extra thought to fuel reserves and availability of daylight. Also, when planning to land away, check the details of the place you propose to visit and ensure that a runway is available for you to land in a direction which is within your own and your aeroplane's crosswind limitations.

Decision making

Decision time is one that calls for self-discipline. As a student you were told where you could — or could not — go, but now you have some freedom of choice. These is no loss of face in abandoning a flight and later you will find that other people will respect you for your ability to make sensible decisions. Do not allow your over-zealous passengers or other pilots to change your mind for you. The verdict is yours and you face the future with it. If the conditions at home are reasonable, but the weather on your intended route is expected to deteriorate, why not fly locally for a short trip, keeping mind and eye on the local conditions?

Decision-making extends beyond your action at the starting point. Very small changes in temperature or wind direction can have noticeable effects on the weather. If you receive a forecast that looks reasonable and you elect to go, but on the way you meet unexpectedly deteriorating conditions, do not press on in the hope that things will get better. If you are on the first outward leg and decide to turn back for home, have a heading already worked out. Take your action early, while you can see where you are and what you are doing. You have learned forced landings with power, but in normal circumstances you can have no excuse for getting yourself in a situation that calls for you to put this exercise to practical use. This is intended only for an emergency and most sensible pilots never meet it in anger. If you treat the weather sensibly, invariably you can return safely to your home aerodrome or have time to divert to another.

The final point to cover here is the case of visiting another place, staying there for a while and then planning to return home. Before you leave your home base, you should obtain a forecast that covers the time of the flight out and the proposed flight back. If all is well at the time but there is a likelihood of deterioration later, either modify the trip or return sooner than you had intended. However, if the weather worsens unexpectedly when you are at your destination and you are worried about getting back, this is the point at which you must exercise your strength as pilot in command of the aeroplane. It may be easier to set out to attempt to return home than to be bold and say that you are not going, but if the new forecast and your common sense tell you even that there *may* be a risk, stay where you are. It may be inconvenient to do this and your passenger may insist that he or she must get back for some reason or another, but you must be firm. Insisting on trying (but failing) to get back for dates, dinners or other appointments must be the biggest single cause of serious accidents to light aircraft; make sure that you are not another example to prove the statistics.

I have laid so much stress on the weather because it is by far the most important aspect to consider wherever and whenever you fly.

On most days in the year it is possible to fly safely and enjoyably. In practice the many varying conditions that you will meet can be sources of both pleasure and education, with different seasons offering their own specialities. Although daylight hours in winter may be few, it is not a time to abandon the thought of flying. I kept a record one January several years ago and noted that I was destined to fly fifteen times in the month. Although some flights needed to be modified only two were cancelled through impossible weather. In the same month in another year I was involved in the seemingly odd task of running a mid-winter fly-in. The air was cold, crisp, clear and calm; and the sun shone. Light aircraft arrived from many directions and one visitor said that it had been the most enjoyable cross-crountry trip that he had experienced for a very long time. At the other end of the calendar scale, spring and summer evenings and autumn days offer some of the best value in pleasure terms. Each of us has his or her own favourite times and conditions, but, to me, flying is irresistible in that final hour of clear summer calm before dark.

Passenger safety
You are responsible for your passengers whilst they are in the aeroplane and whilst they are in the unfamiliar surroundings of the aerodrome. They should not be left alone to wander around as they might wish. They will not know about the hazards of, nor will they see, a revolving propeller. They will not understand that you may not climb on a machine except where a step or walkway is marked. You should tell them which way to enter and leave the cabin; as an example, on most low-wing monoplanes you must climb up from the trailing edge — or the back as they will know it. To walk over the leading edge or front of a wing is an open invitation to walk into the propeller. Especially when your passengers are new to flying, keep the engine stopped while they enter or leave and, before you start it at the beginning of a flight, strap them in, ensure that they are comfortable, and explain what not to touch.

A few people are prone to air-sickness. Sometimes this is a genuine physical condition, but often it is brought on through nervousness. You can minimise the likelihood of this in several ways. Firstly, if conditions are rough and a person has not flown before — especially in a light aeroplane — either suggest delaying to another day or restrict that first flight to a short circuit or two round the aerodrome. Even in calmer weather, fly the aeroplane smoothly and avoid steep turns or other unnecessary manoeuvres. Maintain your companion's attention by pointing to objects of interest and keeping his or her mind working. If the result is relaxed enjoyment, then extend the flight a little, but take care not to overdo it. Someone who is upset in any way on a first flight may not wish to see inside an aeroplane again. That would be a great shame and with sensible care there is no need for that situation to occur. Whatever you do, refrain from trying to display your prowess as an aviator. That is certain to fail.

Rules of airspace
You will have learned where you may and may not go,

keeping clear of airways and other sections of restricted airspace. There is plenty of 'free air' over Britain, so keep within it and do not tempt the possibility of error by going unnecessarily close to forbidden territory. Aerodrome Traffic Zones should be avoided unless you intend to land and you have obtained clearance to enter. None of these restrictions should pose problems, for all areas of special airspace at the heights you are likely to fly are marked on your quarter-million or half-million map.

Choice of chart

This leads to the choice of map — or topographical chart as it is called — for you to use. During your course for the licence, your training centre will have decided which of the two available scales you would use and most probably, for the present, you will continue without changing. However, from now on you have the option to navigate by whichever suits you and your needs; the choice is largely subjective, but not entirely. If you intend to fly fairly long distances in a relatively fast aeroplane, or if you plan to learn to operate radio navigation aids, using the map mainly as a double check, then the half-million is most likely to provide the answer. At the other end of scale, though, in a slow machine on relatively local trips, the detail on the larger scale chart has much to offer and, in addition, provides points of interest that are more than of purely navigational significance. In brief, the half-million provides a relatively uncluttered picture of your route enabling you to concentrate on the main pinpoints, whereas the other gives added information essential for finding small features. Whilst you should not fly in bad weather at this early stage, later you will find the quarter-million chart an invaluable asset when you cannot see far ahead or around you. However, if you fly regularly on one and then change to the other, this may not be quite so straightforward as you expect. There is no real problem, but familiar marks, signs and symbols will be replaced by others that are new to you and distances will seem wrong in relation to time, so give yourself a good clear day on which to try a map conversion flight. Finally, make sure that your maps are the current editions.

Keeping your licence valid

Now that you are a qualified private pilot you must assume the responsibilities that go with the licence. You should keep in reasonably constant flying practice and if you let many weeks pass without getting airborne, have a dual check. The flying centre may insist on this, but if not, ask. It ensures that you remain safe and gives you the chance to smooth any developing rough edges. You must remember also to maintain a valid medical certificate and to arrange for a renewal before the existing one expires. Keep your personal logbook up to date; not only is it a statutory requirement for you do to so, but it becomes an interesting part of your life study in later years. Take especial care to ensure that your licence is valid in terms of flying recency. At present this takes the form of a certificate of test or a certificate of experience that must be signed by an authorised examiner every thirteen months, but this may be changed to a self-renewing pattern. If this is out of order, all insurances including your protection against third part liability could be invalid.

If lack of time or funds, or both, mean that you are unable to fly as often as you would wish, think about ways of putting your restricted resources to work for the best. Flying for five hours on one long flight on a clear summer day is the worst possible way of fulfilling the minimum requirement and the C.A.A. is expected to introduce new criteria to prevent this. Then you will be required to carry out a specific number of flights and, to make what you are able to do more valuable and more enjoyable, you should treat this as the bare minimum. Any flight calls for pre-flight preparation including a look at the meteorological situation, checking on current information (such as NOTAMS), booking out, inspecting the aeroplane, starting, taxying, taking off, general handling and landing. It is important to practise good airmanship such as maintaining a proper lookout and remembering temperatures, pressures and operating speeds.

All this and more will apply in just one circuit of the aerodrome. It is not, therefore, so much the number of hours which matter but the way in which you utilise that time. You must find your own balanced plan, but to prevent long gaps between flights you will be wise to go to the aerodrome fairly frequently and do a couple of circuits, including a practice overshoot (or go-around) from low level. This will keep you in practice and, will keep your mind geared to aviation activities. As you did when you were a student, watch other people flying, talk to fellow pilots if the chance arises, spend a little time in the briefing room and generally absorb the atmosphere.

I am not suggesting that you should remain circuit-bound for the rest of your flying life; far from it. I merely wish to stress the fact that you have no need to fly for a long time and spend a large sum of money on every occasion. Despite comments to the contrary, no pilot is too experienced to gain from a spot of 'circuit bashing' and if you have friends or relatives whom you wish to take into the air with you they will be interested in the various activities involved. If you are restricted to about five hours flying in one year, you might be wise to carry out a short session on the circuit about once a month and use the remaining time for cross-country work. Although facilities vary in different localities, in many areas there are other aerodromes to visit that may be only short distances away, and trips to these are both interesting and beneficial. Although there is a certain aura about long-distance navigation, this may not be a practical possibility for the budget-tied pilot, so you can put your flight-planning and related procedures into practice even if you are flying to a point only a few miles away. If no suitable aerodrome is available, there may be some interesting sights to see from the air and an historic castle may make an interesting destination. Wherever you go and whatever you look at take care: do not indulge in low flying and avoid turning round and round an attraction in a way that may annoy others. Also, do not become obsessed with your visual target to the exclusion of safe flying: without realising, you could tighten your turn and reduce your airspeed to the point of stall or you could lose height continuously while going round with your eyes on the ground. Rememeber, too, to look out for other aircraft. I make no apology for stressing the need to fly safely and sensibly. You may not need warning, but friendly advice now may be appreciated later.

Cost-sharing

In case you fear that your limited funds will put such a severe restraint on your flying that you will be unable to do anything or go anwhere interesting, I have some good news for you. Until now cost-sharing among private pilots has been illegal. Shortly changes in the legislation will allow you to spread *all* the expenses; this covers aircraft hire, fuel, landing fees and all ancilliary matters so long as these are direct operating costs only and there is no element of personal profit for either party. With careful planning you will be able to double the amount of flying your are able to do and it does not preclude the possibility of carrying non-pilots as passengers. On one leg of a cross-country you can be the pilot in charge and your friend alongside you can be gaining some useful navigating experience, and if you use a three- or four-seater a relative or friend can sit behind and enjoy it all. You can land at an aerodrome that might have been out of financial reach if you were paying for everything and there you can change seats to reverse the roles for the second stage. Why not take a qualified pilot friend also when you carry out a couple of circuits at the home base and why not go with him when he goes round? You can help each other and keep each other on the alert for mistakes. There is just one warning point, though. Between you there must be total agreement about who is in charge at any one time. One of you is responsible for the aeroplane and, of course, for making decisions when necessary. So make sure that you settle that before the flight begins.

These are a few general points of advice which I hope will be useful, regardless of your future plans. Whether you wish to fly solely for the pure pleasure of doing so or whether you intend to put an aeroplane to more serious work as a tool for your business travels, you will be wise to remember that a little time spent in becoming accustomed to being an unsupervised pilot will be beneficial. You will be using the same airspace, the same aerodromes and working to the principles and limitations of the same licence, so some standardisation of outlook and attitude now will help to make everything run more smoothly in the future. You will be sharing circuit and approach slots with professional pilots who have many thousands of hours of flying behind them, so you should prepare yourself to fit in to the total aviation system. However, you have nothing to fear, for every pilot goes through this stage and the system has places for us all. Despite all the references to airways, control zones, terminal areas and other alarming-sounding restricted places, most of the air over Britain is free for you to use. You have every opportunity to enjoy the freedom that goes with private flying and we are fortunate to have fewer restrictions on our activities than in many other countries. If we use that freedom sensibly, it will be retained for our future benefit, so every one of us has a duty to fly in a way that will not cause offence. You know how much trouble a single impatient or irresponsible motorist can cause on the roads, so you will realise how much more serious it is when a pilot behaves in a similarly thoughtless manner. Incidentally, flying is much safer than driving, but the results of incautious conduct can be even more devastating.

The next chapter gives brief details of possible courses of action if you wish to gain further qualifications to fly in bad weather or at night, or move towards flying professionally. The chapter after that is set to show you what pleasures are in store if you wish to have a more informal or sporting approach to flying. I suggest, however, that if one idea attracts you more than the other, you should read both, for the more we know about each other's interests and activities, the better. One type of pilot is not superior to the other; each flies for a different reason, while many people happily combine the two.

6
Gaining More Qualifications

As your Private Pilot's Licence with a Group A endorsement enables you to fly any single-engined aeroplane weighing less than 5700 kg (12,500 lb) and to take it anywhere in the world, it carries with it a right to a level of freedom that you are unlikely to put to the full test. Taken to extreme, you could fly a Spitfire to Australia! No one is likely to offer you one in which to do it and, in practice, you would find many problems en route that would make the journey extremely difficult. Equally, you could fly a modern executive single with a retractable undercarriage, a supercharged engine and a variable pitch propeller, or a World War I biplane with a fixed tailskid, no brakes and a rotary engine that has no throttle lever. Clearly, with your limited experience you are not equipped to do any of these things, but it is an encouraging reflection on the level of freedom of the licensing system.

This is where paths tend to diverge. There is a difference between the skills and experience needed to *fly* an aeroplane, which call for that extra attention to handling and airmanship, and *operating* what may be an easy aeroplane to fly, but doing so in poor weather and in more restricted airspace. This chapter is concerned mainly with the second of these options, although as you will see there are several areas of overlap.

Flying by reference to instruments

Whatever you propose to do, unless you intend to restrict your flying to relatively local trips in good weather — and let me make quite clear, there is no harm whatsoever in that — you will need to learn to fly without constant reference to a visual external horizon. The P.P.L. course gives a brief introduction to flight by instruments alone, but this is intended primarily to discourage you from venturing into weather conditions in which you would be unable to cope. You can now build on that knowledge by obtaining specialist tuition and experience in instrument flight, which will enable you to extend your aerial activities. After a course of tuition in the air, with supporting briefings and ground instruction, you will be able to keep the aeroplane in straight and level flight, and do gentle level turns, climbing and descending, both straight and in turns. This will enable you to enter cloud or fly through an area of hazy sky and keep the machine under full control without seeing outside the window. It is not intended as an invitation to launch yourself into a dreary wet, dull day on the basis that there is no need to see what you are doing or where you are going. At this stage, the added experience serves to enable you to penetrate small areas of cloud or haze, but not to persist for long distances through them. You may be able to keep the aeroplane level by instruments alone for considerable periods of time, but remember that without seeing the ground you will be unable to navigate or let-down safely at the end of the flight.

Instrument flight provides a very positive challenge and after learning to handle the aeroplane on the P.P.L. course it is probably the most useful move to make next. Every pilot who goes far from the home circuit, whether flying on business or purely for pleasure, will meet the occasion on which a few minutes of flight by instruments will make the difference between completing a trip or abandoning it. You will be wise to have a few hours of tuition, even if you have no desire — or cannot afford — to indulge in any further formal training beyond that.

At first you may find instrument flying to be tiring, but this is no cause for worry. It does require a good deal of positive concentration and this can lead to tension, revealing itself in lowering standards of performance. Frequent short sessions, interspersed by some more relaxing visual flight, will bring you quite quickly to an acceptable level of competence. Various methods are used to blank your view of the outside world, but usually a hood or visor is placed over your head and if you look straight ahead you can see little more than the panel of instruments in front of you. Do not cheat by seeking odd glimpses of external reality, as this is self defeating and merely lengthens the time taken to reach an acceptable standard; you would be cheating only yourself.

Learning to fly the aeroplane by reference to instruments alone is the essential start to safe flight in all but the best of weather. You must grasp this and be able to switch easily from visual to instrument flight and vice versa, for often the conditions are such that there may be constant changes. However, there are two further stages of achievement that will extend your ability to move about the countryside competently on the days when the weather is not good. The first is to be able to navigate by use of radio aids, by far the most commonly used of which is the Very High Frequency OmniRange, known always as V.O.R. If the aeroplane is equipped with a V.O.R. receiver you can tune in to the appropriate beacon and obtain a radial bearing from it. If you use two V.O.R. stations you can note where the two radials meet and the result gives you a position fix. Another form of available help is a V.H.F. bearing from a radio station that has a direction-finding facility. This has the advantage of being available to any pilot whose aircraft is equppped with normal speech radio and calls for no special kit in the cockpit. In some parts of the country there may not be a station within contact distance, but V.H.F. range is equivalent to a visual sight line and any obstruction between transmitter and receiver blocks the signal, so the higher you fly the greater the chance of success.

By the use of aids you may be able to navigate without constant reference to the ground, but one problem remains: getting down through the weather safely prior to landing at your destination. Fortunately, there are several safe and sensible ways of doing this. Darting downwards through the cloud and hoping that you will emerge at a reasonable height is *not* one. V.O.R. and V.H.F as navigational aids are available also for letting down and there are correct procedures for using these. The services available on speech radio, though, call for comment here, for they vary considerably. The most difficult, but the one in most common civil use, is the V.D.F. (Very High Frequency Direction Finding) let-down, in which the controller gives you a series of bearings from him to you, leaving you to calculate the moves to make in order to follow a prescribed descent pattern. An older and simpler (for the pilot) V.H.F. procedure, which originated in Service aviation and has brought many hundreds of aviators home without mishap, is the Controlled Descent Through Cloud. For many years this was neither recognised by, nor available to, civilians but through an input to the authority by the Aircraft Owners and Pilots' Association (A.O.P.A.), it has become acceptable for use where the controllers are suitably qualified. Unfortunately, only about eight civil aerodromes in the whole of Britain can offer this assistance, but I would certainly opt for it if you should be within aural reach. From a pilot's point of view there is one aid which is even better and that is Precision Approach Radar (a descendant of the original military Ground Controlled Approach) which does almost everything for you except point the aeroplane and control its speed.

Ratings and licences

Fortunately, you have no need to seek a target that is way beyond your reach. There are three levels of skill to attain in instrument flying and each forms a logical step to the next, but if your time, funds and intentions are modest, the first may well suffice. This is the Radio Navigation Certificate. Note that this is a *certificate* and not a *rating*, which means it has no legal or statutory status. It is a symbol of achievement introduced for private pilots by A.O.P.A. but is recognised by the Civil Aviation Authority towards the requirements for the I.M.C. Rating. The latter offers privileges to the holder in terms of permitted visibility and cloudbase minima, and in penetration of certain restricted airspace. This is a very useful qualification to obtain and covers the full needs of all but the most ambitious of pilots who fly privately. At present, it is valid only in U.K. airspace but there is a possibility that it may become a Class 2 Instrument Rating which would give it international status.

Instrument Rating

The third and highest of the qualifications in this group is the Instrument Rating. This is beyond the reach of the majority of private pilots and the privileges that it bestows are beyond their requirements, but the C.A.A. is aware of the need to encourage more people to gain this qualification. There are moves to make substantial reductions in the minimum qualifying hours enabling a pilot to make a steady, unbroken progression from the P.P.L., through the I.M.C. Rating, to the Instrument Rating without losing contact with the training environment. The Instrument Rating is not just a measure of instrument flying ability, for it extends through the full range of operations in controlled airspace such as airways and control zones and covers holding patterns and let-downs. So, the training and test are geared mainly to procedures. The holder of this qualification has access almost anywhere in airspace that is regulated by the civilian authorities.

This may be an appropriate point at which to explain a little about licences and ratings. The licence dictates the purposes for which you may fly. On your Private Pilot's Licence you may not operate for hire or for reward, but you may fly in accordance with any ratings or endorsements that are attached. An Instrument Rating, for example, may be added to a Private Licence or to a Commercial Pilot's Licence and, in each case, the privileges are identical. The only exception is that in the latter the holder may do it on a paid, professional basis. The only other difference is that on a professional licence the rating test must be carried out on a twin-engine aircraft, whilst the private pilot has the option to be trained and tested on a single, although in this case any activities in which an I.R. is needed must be restricted to machines with only one engine.

Night Rating

Although the Instrument Rating is beyond the reach of the majority of private pilots, other useful and interesting qualifications, such as the Night Rating, are easier to achieve. Whilst there may be good reasons for not tackling very long flights at night in a single-engine aeroplane, flying at night can be a most pleasurable experience. Before starting you need a basic grounding in instrument flight, but the course itself consists of a minimum of only five hours by night (including one hour on night navigation) and after a straightforward flying check you become qualified to take passengers with you into the night sky. As you know, conditions vary extensively by day, but they do so even more when the sun has gone down. There may not be a cloud in the sky and the visibility may be almost limitless, but to appreciate the difference between a 'black' night and one with a full moon you can find the answer only by practical experience. If the facility exists at your home aerodrome, I recommend this course very strongly. If it is not, find somewhere else to do it, for it provides an entirely new and invigorating outlook on flying. Almost everywhere, including the larger airports, there is an informal atmosphere that is missing by day and I have heard of only one pilot who has failed to enjoy flying in the dark. Unlike most of the formal qualifications, which need to be maintained by periodical test, the Night Rating is self-renewing. Once it is endorsed on your licence, the only requirement is for you to have completed five take-offs and landings by night within the previous six months. Even if you have gone past that time limit, you may fly five solo circuits and then taxi in to collect your passengers with no need for any paper formalities. This open concession may be varied shortly, however, to prevent those who let years pass without flying at night from taking undue liberties. Do not miss the opportunity to obtain this relatively inexpensive qualification and then use it to increase your flying pleasure. Your passengers, too, will enjoy the experience.

Group B Rating

More expensive to obtain and retain, but satisfying to achieve, is the Group B Rating, which entitles you to fly multi-engine aeroplanes under 5700 kg (12,500 lb). There may be little *practical* point in embarking on this unless you are able to afford or have access to a machine in this category, but, as with all qualifications, the experience in itself can be worthwhile. When I was involved in running a flying school, several people who had trained with us for their private licences saved for a while and underwent twin-engine conversion courses even though they were unlikely to fly twins regularly afterwards. Although I have endeavoured to make clear that this book is not an instruction manual, I would like to emphasise one point about flying an aeroplane with more than one engine. Some people, whether instructors or pilots under instruction, use this course as an excuse to go on trips abroad. This is pointless. Whilst you may find sitting in a larger aeroplane with an engine on each side of you to be a satisfying experience in itself, the purpose of the course is to teach you and give you practice in a new handling experience. Sitting in level flight on a long trip with both engines running is of low value, for once you have synchronised the engines it is little different from being aboard a single. This should be an exercise which takes you back to work on the circuit and in the local area.

A twin *is* different. With one engine shut down and the other at high power, it becomes increasingly apparent, as the

The Piper Navajo is one of the more expensive and complex 'twins' that you may fly on a Group 'B' rating

airspeed decreases, that all the thrust comes from one side. Initially, you will keep straight with firmly increasing rudder pressure, but you will reach a figure at which full rudder is insufficient. If asymmetric power is maintained, the aircraft will then yaw in the direction of the dead engine and, as the wing on the outside will be travelling faster, it will generate more lift and will tend to roll into the 'dead' side. At this point only a reduction in power, probably resulting in a loss of height, will enable you to regain level flight. I mention this briefly because it is the most significant difference between handling an aeroplane with two engines and the single-engine machines to which you have become accustomed. You need to learn the limitations of the twin-engine aeroplane and the basic supporting theory. An ability to handle the machine safely and efficiently on one engine, to let down, take it round the circuit and complete a controlled approach to the runway for an asymmetric landing is the basic purpose of the course and also the main reason for having an aeroplane with more than one engine. Cruising to the continent plays no part in this. Leave that until you have the Group B Rating and then you will be equipped to cope if you have the relatively rare misfortune to suffer an engine failure en route.

Assistant Instructor's Rating

If you enjoy flying and, especially, if you are good at imparting knowledge to others, then you may wish to consider the Assistant Instructor's Rating. You will need to gain a large amount of experience in the air before you begin and you will need to obtain your I.M.C. Rating on the way. One you have obtained this, you should be able to fly as much as you like, and you will not be required to pay for it! The aim of the course is to enable you not just to fly the aeroplane — although you should set yourself a high standard in doing this — but to talk sensibly at the same time. If you are to teach a new manoeuvre to a student, you must be able to convince him by ensuring that things happen when you say they are happening. It is easy to get out of phase.

What you plan to say may take longer than the flight sequence, or vice versa. Previously, instructors were taught to recite precise 'patter', but now an individual is encouraged to find his own way of delivering the message. Most of the flying part of the course is devoted to this, but naturally there is a need to learn supporting theory and also to be able to teach on the ground. A student can assimilate far more in the quiet of the briefing room than he is able to absorb in the cockpit, so an instructor must be able to explain points clearly and concisely to avoid subsequent confusion in the air. After giving a flying lesson, an instructor's ability to point out what happened during the flight is equally important.

An assistant instructor is required to operate under the supervision of a more experienced mentor who holds a full Instructor's Rating. All flights must be authorised by the more senior person, but once in the air there is no one to lean over the newcomer's shoulder, so anyone who aspires to teach flying and all that goes with it should think hard about what this involves. The standards of private flying generally are dictated largely by the standards of the people who carry out the training. An assistant instructor should not fly just to amass more hours for himself so that he can qualify later for a senior licence (even though the licensing regulations are inclined to encourage just that). Anyone who teaches flying should have a devotion to duty for similar reasons to that of a doctor, who is expected to know the possible results of his failure to do his very best. A pilot should become an instructor only if he has a desire and a natural ability to teach others, and if those qualities exist, he is well set on the road to success.

At present an instructor or assistant instructor may add his or her rating to a Private Pilot's Licence, but to bring the U.K. into line internationally, a plan for the future is the introduction of a Basic Commercial Pilot's Licence, valid for aerial work (which covers instructing, crop spraying, pipeline inspection etc.) but not for public transport of passengers. There will be a C.P.L. written examination and a minimum requirement of 200 hours as a pilot. If the C.A.A.'s present plans mature, it will remain possible for a person to add an Assistant Instructor's Rating to a P.P.L. so long as no remuneration is given, but for a paid pilot the new B.C.P.L. will be a necessity. A candidate for an assistant instructor's course qualifying by the P.P.L. route will need a minimum of 150 hours as first pilot, whereas one who has taken the necessary training to obtain the B.C.P.L. will be able to start his specialised course at 100 hours P.I.C. Either way the course for the assistant instructor's rating requires a minimum of 28 hours flying and associated ground tuition.

Commerical Pilot's Licence and Instrument Rating

If you wish to fly as a passenger-carrying professional pilot, two distinctive and very different ways are open. The first is to attend a full-time course of training for the Commerical Pilot's Licence and Instrument Rating. This must be carried out at a school approved for the purpose by the Civil Aviation Authority and only three of these exist in the United Kingdom. The cost of such a venture is far beyond the financial means of most people, and the only way of entering this system is to be selected and sponsored by an airline or other aircraft operating organisation. There are several ways in which this is tackled and in many cases some personal financial contribution is required, while in others a partial repayment is expected later in the form of a reduced salary for an agreed number of years; or there may be a combination of the two. The scope for joining the profession via sponsorship depends entirely on the market of the moment. Almost throughout the history of aviation there has been either a shortage or a surplus of pilots and periods of stability in the supply and demand position are rare. In the early eighties there have been few job vacancies and airlines have not needed to sponsor new candidates, but a recent programme of research into the industry's needs shows that, pending retirements and related factors, there will be a steady increase in the number of available opportunities.

The alternative mode of entry is known to some as the 'back-door' method. If you do not go via the route of the new

Basic C.P.L. you can obtain exemption from attendance on an approved course if you amass 700 hours of flying before you apply to the C.A.A. for a full Commercial Pilot's Licence. You are required to pass similar tests and examinations before you can qualify but, as you will not have been groomed by specialists on the way, you will need personal initiative in order to attain the standards required.

Several correspondence schools sell postal courses, while other establishments offer ground tuition in the classroom. The choice may depend on where you live and how you can allocate your time, but in the profession there are differing opinions on which is the better way to proceed. A compromise may provide the answer, such as a home-study course (enabling you to gain a basic knowledge in your own time and at your own personal pace) combined with a short and concentrated period at a school shortly before you take the written examinations. All these organisations advertise regularly in aviation magazines.

Whilst tuition covering the syllabus for the ground examination may be available readily and at fairly modest prices, the problem lies in obtaining the required flying experience. In the early stages there is unlikely to be any alternative to paying your own way, for until you have reasonable experience in the air no one will be willing to put you to work on their behalf. It is important to realise that you are not permitted to receive any reward, whether financially or in kind, for your services as a private pilot. However, as your aim is to obtain flying, this is unlikely to be a deterrent. Remember, though, that you will be able to share expenses with another pilot when hiring an aeroplane.

I have come across several determined aspirants to flying careers finding ways of gaining experience. One relative novice made a regular practice of ferrying club aircraft to and from the home aerodrome and a maintenance organisation. Another persuaded the local gliding club to allow him to tow some of the more experienced members into the air, becoming progressively more useful and towing the less qualified glider pilots as his own experience and expertise increased. Yet another, by powerful persuasion, convinced private owners that they should have chances to see their own aircraft in the air. The most generally-used method, once the necessary minimum experience has been obtained (currently 150 hours as first pilot and possession of an I.M.C. Rating), is to undergo a course to qualify for the Assistant Instructors Rating, details of which I have explained already. Although this is by far the most straightforward way of obtaining all the hours needed subsequently, I repeat my earlier advice that, as an instructor, you have a responsibility that is geared closely to the standards of future pilots, so make sure that you tackle the task conscientiously and are not guilty of being just an hour-piler.

Professional flying

Professional flying comes in many forms. If you ask most people what this covers they will assume that your refer to the work of an airline pilot. This is understandable, for this is the face that the public sees, but there are several other aerial activities that come into this category. Pilots earn their livings by spraying or dusting crops from light single-engine aeroplanes; others fly light twins on taxi, charter or executive work; some (often to gain more experience) fly passengers on round-the-pier pleasure flights from holiday resorts, or round the sights of the local area from many aerodromes, or at special events where large crowds gather, such as flying displays. Even airline flying does not fall into one single groove. Many pilots working for a national carrier on long-haul routes operate one trip out, have a break, return the aeroplane and then take some leave. They may complete only four or five flights in a month and derive very little pleasure from the work. In fact, following earlier intensive medical studies in pilot workload among the airlines the modern airliner has become automated to the extent that the current worry centres on the level of inactivity, which can lead to boredom. Compare this with the task of the pilot who flies scheduled services on short hops between the Scottish islands, with high ground, rapidly changing weather, often small airfields and a workload that keeps him 'on the go' all the time. It may lack glamour, but it is flying, and we should not overlook a person's initial reason for becoming involved with aeroplanes, which, presumably, was to fly! At present there are three U.K. professional pilot licences. The first, the Commercial Pilot's Licence, suffices for all aerial work and passenger carrying on smaller aircraft. An Instrument Rating may be added. The second is the Senior Commerical Pilot's Licence, but this is due to be phased out shortly. The top qualification is the Airline Transport Pilot's Licence, which is precisely what its name implies, calling for a written examination of a higher standard than that for the C.P.L., an Instrument Rating and a minimum of 1500 hours flying experience. When the (aerial work) C.P.L. is introduced, the three experience and achievement levels will be retained. Many people have no desire to fly professionally and there is much to be said for keeping flying purely as a pastime.

Apart from obtaining one or more of the advanced qualifications that I have mentioned in this chapter, there is a completely different route open to you if you wish to enjoy flying for its own sake. For many of the activities available, you need add no ratings to your licence.

7
Purely For Pleasure

Shortly after obtaining your licence you may wish to take your family and friends on local flights from your home aerodrome, or you may venture on some longer trips on a cost-sharing basis with other private pilots. No two airports or aerodromes are alike, so take a look at all that are within easy financial and navigational reach. Fairly quickly you will discover which you like and which you wish to avoid. Reception and available facilities range from excellent to non-existent, and the landing fees payable in no way measure the benefits to be derived. Some places have worthwhile reductions in charges for cash payment and others lower their prices at certain times, so make notes of these for future use.

Visiting other Aerodromes

Growing attention has been given to the relationship between pilots and aerodromes. Any system is only as good or as bad as the people who operate it, with the result that some airfields and some users are unable to come to mutually acceptable terms. There are two angles to every story, so I would be out of order to say that the aerodromes are always wrong and the pilots cannot fail to be right. There are some pilots who rock the system in various ways and I must stress that improved relationships will emerge only if everybody endeavours to play ball. There is the person who fails to follow the correct procedure in the circuit pattern; the individual who is told that one runway is in use, states his intention of using it and then appears on final approach on a different heading; the impatient user who cannot control his temperament, usually finishing his flight by taxying dangerously fast and disregarding everything and everybody; the pilot who seeks and obtains permission to enter a busy runway for take-off and then sits there with his back to the approach carrying out his checks, causing delays to all

There are several versions of the rugged Auster family and all require handling — especially when landing

others; the extrovert who cannot fly without needing to show how clever he is, to the justified annoyance of everyone else; the time-waster who demands more than a reasonable amount of attention from the various services that may be available and many others who harm the good name of private flying to spoil it for the silent majority.

Aerodromes should be there to be used, but many are private property and, except at places with public use licences, they are not automatically available to everyone. Some aerodromes offer a genuine welcome, supported by good service facilities at reasonable prices. Others are quite the opposite and some even resent private pilots in light aircraft.

Assistance from controllers
There have been extensive discussions within the flying fraternity and among controllers regarding the assistance that a controller should be expected to give a novice pilot. The most obvious case is that of the choice of runway. The one in use may be long with approach aids and be generally suitable for larger aircraft, but it may be markedly out of wind. Another runway may be available that would be more suitable for use by light aircraft. Should the pilot be expected to ask for the into-wind heading or should the controller anticipate the need and offer it? Clearly opinions differ, but a

student or new P.P.L. holder may be reluctant to ask for something special and may be tempted to land, quite unnecessarily, in conditions that are beyond his or the aircraft's crosswind limits. An experienced aviator would stand no nonsense and refuse the heading. A little thoughtful anticipation from the tower can make the novice pilot feel much more at ease. Check carefully before you go anywhere to ensure that you will be able to land and take-off without serious crosswind problems and if a suitable alternative runway is available make it clear that you wish to use it.

Aerodrome management and controllers should be there to help and encourage users and most of them do. There are, however, a growing number of places that have become self-styled airports and have lost touch with the reason for their existence. I could quote several; one manager expressed a wish for flying clubs to stop sending students to his hallowed field on their cross-country exercises, for they make mistakes in his traffic zone and get in the way of the real pilots; at another, relatively small, aerodrome with barely sufficient movements to justify its existence, aircraft without radio are refused permission to land. I would have expected the management of such a sadly under-used facility to seek more traffic, particularly as any landing fee adds to the inward cashflow, whether it comes from a machine with a cockpit full of sophisticated aids or from a basic aeroplane with no frills. I find it strange that aerodrome managers who complain about hard times should wilfully refuse any possible income from this substantial source.

I mention all this because you can make your flying far more enjoyable if you establish sound working relationships with those aerodromes which you are likely to use regularly. In the main, the smaller the aerodrome, the more informal and friendly it will be, but there are some marked exceptions and a few of the larger airports have very good reputations among the private flying fraternity. Everything revolves round attitude of mind, for large airliners on scheduled services can mix happily with light aeroplanes. Some airports have general aviation terminals where all the facilities are separated from those used by the bigger brethren.

Private airstrips

If you wish to get away from all the formality of established airports and the larger aerodromes, there are several private unlicensed airfields and hundreds of private airstrips. A few aircraft insurance policies do, however, exclude these from cover. Many of these fields are small and some have trees or power lines in awkward places, so extra caution may be needed. If in doubt, a visit by road and a good visual inspection on foot may prove of value. Until 1987, it was illegal to be given dual instruction, or even advice from another pilot sitting beside you, when operating into or out of an unlicensed field. Clearly, this was an invitation to low safety standards and following pressure spearheaded by the Aircraft Owners' and Pilots' Association, the Civil Aviation Authority has rectified the omission (see Article 71 of the Air Navigation Order). If you fly into one of these smaller or more difficult sites, you may be wise to have some guidance from an instructor or from an experienced pilot who has knowledge of the place and the best ways in which to use it. A private airstrip, of course, is as private as your own garden, so make sure that you seek and obtain permission beforehand. Many owners do, however, encourage and

A private landing strip — away from the formalities of a licensed aerodrome — holds its own attractions. A Tiger Moth fits well into the atmosphere.

welcome visitors. There is something intangible but very satisfying from operating an aeroplane in or out of a field that is not a conventional airport or aerodrome. If the chance arises, try it.

Use of radio

Almost certainly you will have learned to use the radio as an integral part of your flying course and you will hold a restricted Radiotelephony Licence, allowing you to operate an aeroplane's V.H.F. equipment. With practice and experience you will be able to put this asset to increasing use, but do not depend on it as a foolproof substitute for your own thinking and planning. Recently, I heard about an instrument rated pilot who was on a carefully planned flight from beacon to beacon when his aircraft suffered a total electrical failure. The weather was reasonable, but he was on the verge of panic, for he had not navigated by visual means since qualifying for his P.P.L. five years previously. He had learned to fly solely so that he could travel on business and he had undergone a neat series of pre-packed courses that enabled him to operate very efficiently in an all-avionics environment and in an assortment of conditions. Fortunately, another pilot with a broader background was with him and he continued the flight to the intended destination by looking out of the windows. Every pilot should be able to do that; apart from the need to cope if the aids fail, there is much to be gained from the peace and isolated contentment that go with radio silence. Radio and the gear that goes with it are there to be used to full advantage, but take care not to allow your ears to take over from your eyes. Much of the most enjoyable flying takes place where no radio is available.

Rallies and competitions

Various aviation functions are staged all over the British Isles and on the Continent, and you will find these enjoyable and interesting to attend. Most flying displays take place from aerodromes that accept visiting aircraft up to a certain cut-off time before the show starts. You may not be permitted to leave until the display is over, although some organisers include departure slots in their programme for the benefits of those who must get away earlier. If you are hiring a club aircraft, you will be wise to check that its availability and the arrival/departure times are compatible. Gather a friend or two to go with you, watch the show and then fly back again afterwards and you have the basis of a very pleasant day out.

Your own flying club may hold home-based competitions. These can cover a wide scale of activities and they can be both enjoyable and benficial to your future flying. A navigation test, calling for both skill and initiative, or a forced landing contest will check your abilities against those of your fellow fliers and will help you to maintain a good standard. Many pilots dismiss circuit flying as something to leave behind from their students days and, equally, many consider forced landings to be nothing more than exercises necessary to pass the general flying test for the P.P.L. Everything that you were required to learn and practise for the licence has a place in your subsequent flying, so why not keep up to scratch on the basics and enjoy the competitive element?

Fly-ins
There are fly-ins and other functions organised regularly throughout the summer season. Some of these are very small and very informal, while others attract large numbers of aircraft of many types together with an equally interesting variety of people. If you trained at an airport and know only hard runways, taxi-ways and large tarmac or concrete aprons, a flight to an event at a small grass aerodrome operated by a flying club offers a new experience. Conversely, of course, if you have trained and carried out most of your subsequent flying from a small place, you should not wait too long before you take yourself into an airport. There is nothing to fear. Just ensure that you plan properly in advance and that you understand the procedures that you are required to follow.

The larger and more organised events that you can attend are staged by national bodies such as the Vintage Aircraft

Although surviving from World War II, Tiger Moths exist in considerable numbers and are ideal for pilots wishing to convert to 'tail-draggers'

Club and the Popular Flying Association. The latter's annual three-day rally in June is an event that every private pilot should experience. Frequently, a thousand or more light aircraft attend at some stage during the long weekend. If you think that light aviation is made up solely of Pipers, Cessnas and similar products, then the P.F.A. rally is a 'must' for you. Dozens of different types, hundreds with no radio, all supported with a living atmosphere of enthusiasm for flying, continue to make this a unique and unforgettable occasion on the British aviation calendar. It places flying for fun in its rightful perspective.

Rallying

The word rally may be used to cover almost any type of aviation event, but some functions are more specific and 'rallying' is a definite form of flying activity. Apart from a concours d'élégance or a spot landing test, there may be a competition involving a specified route where the main requirements are accuracy in both map reading and timekeeping. The details of the route may be published well in advance or announced at short notice. An extension of this is a requirement for a tightly-timed arrival over one or more points that are close to the destination aerodrome. There may be a flight planning competition, which includes a check on the navigational equipment used. There are many variations and the activities of the precision pilots are among those that fall into the rally category. They all serve to make your flying more pleasurable and to improve your level of performance as a pilot.

Rallies are popular events enabling pilots to get to know each other. This rally is at Sywell in Northamptonshire.

Flying to the Continent

Flying to the continent may be among your aeronautical ambitions. If you are based in the south, the most obvious and frequently-used destination is le Touquet on the north French coast. Although it is close to England and is therefore not a long, expensive flight, you will gain all the relevant experience of passing through customs, flight planning, being sensibly equipped to cross the water (and this really is important) and landing away from Britain. Le Touquet is ideal not only on geographical grounds, but also because the management and controllers are very receptive to visiting pilots and make newcomers feel at ease. This airport was granted a special A.O.P.A. award in 1985 on behalf of the many hundreds of private pilots who had used it in the previous year.

When you fly to or on the continent, make sure that you check and take careful note of the forecast weather, especially if you are venturing into the mountainous regions. The use of weather sense is always important, but when flying overseas added attention to detail will ensure safety. In addition to visiting interesting places, there are opportunities to attend various European rallies. These vary greatly; some are heavily socially orientated, with the flying being of secondary significance, while others are more pilot-centred and more competitive. Before committing yourself to the time and expense of entering such an event, study the paperwork to discover whether it is right for you.

Flying different types of aircraft

If you wish to try something different such as flying other types of aircraft there is no need to travel far and you may not need to move from your own home aerodrome. Many machines are primarily functional in that they may be ideal for touring purposes, but they lack any feel or spirit. If you trained on a Cessna 152, and then convert to, perhaps, a Cessna 172 to enable you to take more people with you, this is a logical step in terms of personal transportation, so if the opportunity exists, take it. However, I am looking more towards your conversion onto aeroplanes that are enjoyable to fly for the pure pleasure of being in the air. The A to B tourer and the sporting mount are very different aircraft, while a vintage type has something very special to offer so try to become introduced to one or more of these less common machines.

Although the basic principles of flight apply to all aeroplanes, some are more critical than others in certain phases. The most noticeable difference lies between the type with today's conventional tricycle or nose-wheel undercarriage and the 'tail-dragger'. If you trained on the former, you will need some instruction before attempting the latter.

Differences between tricycle and tail-down machines
There are several reasons for this, and they go further than the obvious variations in attitude when on the ground. The operating techniques on the tail-down types call for more accuracy of handling and judgment, as on take-off the aircraft must be 'flown' into the take-off attitude and on landing the hold-off between the approach angle and the three-point attitude for touchdown needs considerable practice and experience. It is essential that you should understand the differences before you fly 'tail-draggers'.

On the tricycle type the aircraft's centre of gravity lies ahead of the mainwheels so that it sits steadily on its nosewheel. With the tail-down machine the centre of gravity must lie behind the mainwheels to enable it to sit on its tailwheel or tailskid. This has an effect on handling, especially during the landing run. An aeroplane acts rather like a weather-vane and, because of the large keel area to the rear (including the fin and rudder), it will always try to head into wind. This is especially marked on the tail-down type and, as the rudder is partly blanketed when the machine is on three points, some energetic exercise with the feet may be needed to keep straight when speed reduces towards the end of a landing run. If the runway or strip is out of wind, the aircraft will tend to veer off into the direction from which the wind is coming, so quick reaction is essential to catch it almost before it starts to go. Over correction, too, is a possibility, causing a swing to start in the opposite way. Difficulty occurs when a swing has been allowed to develop beyond a point of easy correction and this is where the weight behind the main-wheels comes into force. It will move forwards and continue to do so, causing the aircraft to turn more rapidly as the weight gets ahead of the mainwheels. By this stage no amount of work on the pilot's part will make the aircraft run straight again, so one must sit tight and await the subsequent embarrassment. You have heard of a ground loop and may have wondered what it is; now you know!

All this offers an interesting and intriguing challenge. A complete pilot will not wish to restrict his flying activities to everything that is easy, for there is a lot to learn and the experience that you will pick up on the way will prove both valuable and enjoyable. If circuit flying in a tricycle type has lost its excitement for you, your first session of take-offs and landings in the taildragger will prove very refreshing! Taxying calls for more caution, with constant weaving of the nose as it is in the way of your forward vision; due to gyroscopic effect, there will be a tendency to swing on take-off when the tail comes up; speed on the approach will be more critical if the hold-off is to be accurate, the three-point touchdown will call for good judgment; and, as I have explained, there is a need to work to keep straight on the landing run.

You may wonder where and how you can find a suitable aeroplane on which to learn these skills, but in most parts of the country this should be possible. Although each individual type exists in relatively small numbers, there are numerous machines in the tail-down category. Several versions of the Jodel are on the U.K. register, dozens of ex-R.A.F. Chipmunks are spread throughout Britain and there are numerous Tiger Moths, and there is at least one flying club still conducting all basic flying training on them.

Vintage aeroplanes

If you have the opportunity of an introduction to a brakeless biplane fitted with a tailskid, such as the Tiger Moth, it will be an entirely new aviation experience for you and will give you an insight into a form of flying that has something special to offer. It is preferable not to start in the very coldest weather, for you will need protection from the slipstream and from the many draughts that will creep in and around you, all of which can be very welcome on a warm summer day. If the wind and the noise act as a deterrent on your first flight, do not give up. Almost everyone who has converted from a modern 'spamcan' to a vintage biplane has enjoyed it

Replicas of military aircraft are becoming popular. This is a scaled down Focke Wulf FW 190 German fighter of World War II.

and many have refused to revert to their earlier comfort levels. Apart from the effects of the tail-down ground attitude, other variations in flying technique will come to the fore; you may be accustomed to carrying out turns almost by aileron alone, using only a minimal touch of rudder to maintain balance. Try that in most biplanes and the wing will go down, but the aircraft will not turn. On some of the earlier designs the aeroplane will tend to yaw in the wrong direction, as the drag caused by the downgoing aileron will be greater than that caused by the upgoing control. On modern machines with differential ailerons the drag problem has been virtually eliminated, but on the early biplanes you will need to work to co-ordinate the use of feet and hands to produce an acceptably clean turn.

Flying a vintage biplane on a calm, clear, summer evening is the most satisfying of pastimes, but make sure that you receive some proper tuition in handling and airmanship (think: how do we taxi without brakes?) before you try to cope with a machine that has such markedly different characteristics from those to which you are accustomed.

Aerobatics

Many people are under the impression that anyone who flies solely for the pleasure of flying must indulge in large doses of aerobatics. This is not so. There are many delights in store for the pilot who restricts his activities to erect flight, but if you have an inclination to perform loops, rolls and other manoeuvres, then you have neither need nor reason to quash that enthusiasm. However, as in all new activities, you must not try to do it on a teach-yourself basis. You should receive tuition from an instructor who is experienced in the art and you must use an aeroplane with a Certificate of Airworthiness in the Aerobatic category. Most probably you

The Christen Eagle — here seen under construction — is a small biplane geared to the needs of the specialist aerobatic pilot

have not learned or practised spinning and recovery, but you must become proficient in this before indulging in aerobatic manoeuvres. Whilst learning and practising aerobatics, you will make many mistakes, so not only must you be able to recognise and recover from a spin, but you must have adequate air beneath you in which to sort the situation. In short, climb to a sensible height for all manoeuvres. Until you are very experienced and competent, low level aerobatics can be extremely dangerous.

If you are fortunate enough to be able to choose the type of aeroplane on which you learn your loops, rools and variations, the following points may be of interest. The machine most commonly used at flying schools is the Cessna 150 or 152 Acrobat. This is quite suitable for training in the basic exercises, but it lacks the lustre of some of the more lively machines. I am not a dedicated aerobatic pilot, but I have enjoyed many manoeuvres in Chipmunks. The type has a solid, crisp feel and handles as though bigger, heavier and more powerful than it is. Leisurely slow rolls are a particular pleasure in this former military trainer. I say 'former' because almost all the civil examples now flying were built for and used by the Services and were released for sale when only smaller numbers were required to be retained. (Incidentally, the Chipmunk's virtues are such that it entered Royal Air Force service as long ago as 1950; currently it is the only aeroplane in use with all three British Services and it is destined to remain in military use until the year 2000.) There are several other types, including some rather special machines geared to the needs of aerobatic contests, such as the French CAP 10 and 20, or the variations of the diminutive Pitts biplanes. However, your immediate needs will be more modest and you may find that you have access to a Belgian Stampe SV4 or a British Tiger Moth. Although both are biplanes and broadly similar in appearance, these two types are very different in handling qualities. The Stampe performs relatively smoothly and flies like a monoplane, while the Tiger requires some very hard work if you are to achieve success. If you can roll a Tiger Moth, all the other types will seem simple, so that makes it an excellent trainer.

There is no need to commit yourself to a long and expensive course in aerobatics, as you can book a short familiarisation flight to discover what it is all about. I must repeat, though, that it is unsafe to carry out your own experiments without proper guidance. You must receive instruction from a qualified instructor in a suitable aerobatic aeroplane.

A monoplane for the keen aerobatic pilot is the French-built CAP 20

Air racing

An activity that attracts relatively few pilots is air racing. This may be out of reach of the majority of people, for almost certainly flying schools and clubs will not allow their machines to be entered, although I know of cases where exceptions have been made. For this you need 100 hours of first pilot time and a Competitor's Licence issued by the Royal Aero Club, so it may be a distant target if you have qualified for your licence fairly recently. However, it is a pastime not to be spurned or forgotten. In the past I was fortunate enough to be able to compete in a number of races — even being the last person past the post can be enjoyable!

If an air race is to be worthwhile it must have some formality. All the relevant details of your aeroplane must be stated clearly on the entry form and you must appear, with your machine, well ahead of the start of the event. This is to enable the handicappers to compute your take-off time, in relation to the other aircraft, and for the scrutineers to examine your machine for any deviations from standard. In this way, fast and slow aeroplanes can compete in the same event and, in theory, all should meet at the finishing line. The tense moments spent sitting with your engine running and waiting for the starter's flag to drop just for you; the turn round the pylon at the scatter point to get you onto the first full leg of the circuit; the decision to fly low on an into-wind leg and whether it is worth losing speed to climb to benefit from a section of the course on which the wind is behind you; the way in which you tackle the many pylon turns and how you organise your descent on the final run-in to the

The diminutive Cassutt is a specialist machine for closed circuit class races

finish. All these, interspersed with frequent visual flashes around the cockpit to check engine r.p.m., oil pressure and oil temperature, combine to make up a level of intensive activity that makes racing what it is. There are many variations on race patterns: short closed circuits and long hauls, scratch races and specialised events for machines that conform to a specific race formula. If you enjoy handling your aeroplane, the short closed circuit races have much to offer.

Precision flying

A relatively recent introduction to Britain, and one that requires neither vast resources nor great experience, is precision flying, which started in Scandinavia in 1973 as aerial orienteering. The aim is to measure and improve a pilot's skills in flight planning, accuracy of navigation, in-flight observation and precise landings. Competitions are held for pilots flying solo in single-engine aircraft, without using radio navigation aids or electronic calculators. The emphasis is on basic piloting skills with traditional instruments, map reading and observation. Each competition comprises a flight-planning test, a cross-country exercise of about 45 nautical miles, with photographic and ground targets to be identified, and three spot landings. Any machine with a cruising speed between 65 and 90 knots may be used and each entrant states his intended cruising speed, which must be in a multiple of 5 knots between these two limits.

At the start, each competitor is given a $\frac{1}{4}$ million chart, a set of photographs, instructions, flight planning forms and departure and arrival charts. He is required to compute a heading to within two degrees and to state the planned time on the leg to within five seconds. 30 minutes are allowed for this part of the exercise and the whole operation is carried out to a tight timing schedule. Wheels rolling for take-off must be exactly one hour after the entrant received the instructions. At the end, the landing tests are all different, such as a normal landing with power and flaps (even side-slipping is allowed), a glide approach from 1000 feet (with no use of power but flaps are permitted), and an obstacle landing over a bunting, two metres high, placed fifty metres before the touch-down point. These contests are growing in popularity among private pilots and are organised on a regular basis by the British Precision Pilots' Association. As a relatively inexperienced flier you can tackle this and it is a proven way of sharpening skills and standards. A big attraction is that the cost is minimal and normal club aeroplanes are ideally suited to the task.

Gliding

Although my intention is to explain which outlets are open to you to put your Private Pilot's Licence to enjoyble use, I would be wrong not to refer to gliding. You do not need a

To fly a self-launching motor glider you require a separate rating on your licence. This is the Grob G109 motor glider.

licence to fly a glider. However, your basic piloting skills apply whether or not a machine is powered, for the controls work in the same manner, the wind and the weather affect both and the airspace is shared equally. Some gliding clubs have efficient tailor-made courses for power pilots, while others look askance at anyone who has needed an engine in front to keep himself in the air. My advice is to explain that you have a P.P.L., but that you know nothing about the art of unpowered flight and you wish to learn. There *are* differences and I learned these the hard way.

When I was young I joined a gliding club in Scotland. At the time I was serving as a pilot in the Royal Air Force and several years previously I had carried out a little gliding as a cadet in the Air Training Corps. With youthful arrogance, I expected to be given a quick check circuit and sent solo, but not so. I was given ground tuition in handling, effects of controls in the air, turning, stalling and then a session of winch-launched circuits. I should have been much more humble in my attitude to the new task, as later I realised the need for an open approach to learning a new set of practices and procedures. A few years later I converted several glider pilots to power flying for their P.P.L.s and I was pleasantly surprised to find that their handling standards and their knowledge of the elements put most power pilots to shame. So remember not to go to a gliding club with the thought that you know all about it, but with a willingness to learn. Use your previous flying experience in a way that will enable you to cope with the different demands of a glider.

The British Gliding Association is the controlling body and there are clubs all over Britain. Gliders can be winch-launched or aero-towed to a height, but the aim of the glider pilot is not to be pulled up just to go down again. His purpose is to seek, find and use thermals (rising currents of air) to gain height without the need for man-made power. Many clubs offer temporary membership and some arrange special weekend or weekday courses for conversion purposes. Launch prices are reasonable and you will not need to break too heavily into your bank account to discover whether or not gliding is for you.

Motor-gliders
A logical extension of this is the self-launching motor glider, which by definition calls for a machine with a weight not exceeding 1650 lb (750 kg) and a maximum stalling speed of 40 knots. Also, there are certain restrictions on the amount of fuel that may be carried, on wing span, rate of climb and so on, but with an overrriding need for a minimum normal glide ratio of 20 to 1, providing the main differences between this and the conventional light aeroplane. It is precisely what its name implies in that it can fly effectively with engine on or engine off, becoming a sailplane when in the latter condition. As one who knows from experience, Bill Bowker, who operates a Grob 109 from Rush Green, near Hitchin in Hertfordshire, tells you more than I can hope to cover, so the next six paragraphs are his words.

'Although the definition is interpreted fairly loosely in current designs, the result is a class of machine with great charm and attraction for both power and glider pilots.

Proficiency on the type can be achieved by approaching from either a power or gliding direction, or by starting from scratch and training *ab initio* on an S.L.M.G. The experience required is close to that needed for a Group A P.P.L., and a conversion can readily be made either way. Note however that a separate test is needed for S.L.M.G. and Group A Landplanes, as one group does not automatically include the other. To qualify for an S.L.M.G. licence from a good gliding qualification takes a little longer than from a P.P.L., but it is a logical and fairly readily accomplished step. Instructors who wish to examine and test candidates for an S.L.M.G. rating must be licensed accordingly. The British Gliding Association can recommend instructors to the C.A.A. for this qualification; others with appropriate experience can apply to the C.A.A. direct. A Restricted Motor Glider Instructor's Rating is available for those wishing to give instruction only in gliding in an S.L.M.G.

The particular attention of the S.L.M.G. to both glider and power pilots is its unique ability to take off, climb, and then at an appropriate height, dispense with its engine. In the hands of an experienced glider pilot and in reasonable gliding conditions height can be gained and maintained as in a medium performance sailplane. To a power pilot the first experience of sustained flight with the propeller stopped is sensational.

Other attractions, for those from a power background, are the respectable cross-country performance with lower power and good economy, the comfort and low noise level, and the convenience of folding wings. The saving in fuel and hangarage costs compared with a conventional light aircraft can be considerable, too.

On the other hand it is necessary to appreciate certain disadvantages of the S.L.M.G. when compared with more popular types. Having high aspect ratio wings of considerable span and a relatively small engine with a short fast turning propeller, acceleration on take off is slow and substantially affected by the state of the runway surface and gradient. Soggy wet grass is bad news for motor gliders. Taxy with great care if you are more accustomed to ordinary light aircraft of 30 to 40 ft wing span. Motor gliders come like sailplanes in this respect with 50 to 60 ft wings and little ground clearance. Apart from the extra roll inertia of the high aspect ratio wing, and the slow acceleration all the way up to cruising speed, the main difference for the power pilot is the use of airbrakes instead of flaps, (no lift, all drag), and the often rather quaint pitch change mechanism for the two position propeller. Glider airframes are very clean and have considerable energy when approaching at, for example 60 knots. Short field operation is entirely feasible, but fine judgement with the airbrake lever is required.

Apart from the remarkable cross-country performance, the Grob G109B, for example, can cruise for 5 to 6 hours at 90 to 100 knots using 3 gals per hour comfortably sprung between glass and carbon fibre aerofoils, while a big attraction for P.P.L. pilots is the opportunity to learn gliding skills. For this aspect of S.L.M.G. operation go to a gliding club or school and talk to a suitably rated B.G.A. instructor. The gliding performance of a modern S.L.M.G. may not be up to competition standard, but it is quite useful if you know what you are doing. Gliding goals are interesting and achievable in easy stages with proper instruction, and provide satisfying pleasure and sport flying for those not looking to progress their P.P.L. into I.M.C., night and twin ratings.

Microlights

Microlights offer another outlet for your enthusiasm for the freedom of flight. These mini-aeroplanes come in two distinct forms: those with three-axis controls which operate in the same way as conventional aeriplanes, and those that are manoeuvred by the weightshift method. Because these are markedly different from other forms of flying machine, I refer again to the words of one with specialist knowledge and experience. In this case John Fack, the Managing Director of Pegasus Flight Training, takes up the tale . . .

'Flying weightshift? You won't catch me flying one of those! The controls are different'. A common enough response, you might suppose, from stick and rudder pilots

when confronted with the opportunity of committing aviation in a modern 2-seat weightshift microlight aircraft. They
are the unlucky ones. The more fortunate open their minds,
don their flying suits, and take to the air to discover the
pleasures of good old fashioned open air flying.

Microlights have progressed significantly in the last five
years. A modern two-seater cruises at 60 m.p.h., has a
maxium level speed of 85 m.p.h., climbs at 600 feet per
minute, two up, lands in 150 yards, rigs in 30 minutes, is
stored in a garage, uses 2 gallons per hour, and provides
many hours of safe, economical flying. It runs on a Permit to
Fly, renewable annually. Developments are such that microlights no longer crawl about the sky making an infernal
noise, but provide genuine cross-country performance at a
realistic price and, in the case of the new water-cooled
Pegasus Flash II, at a noise level lower than any other
aeroplane. So what should a P.P.L. 'A' holder do if he wants
to join weight-shift pilots?

Legally speaking, nothing. A P.P.L. permits you to fly a
microlight without further qualifications. It makes sense,
however, to embark on a conversion course at a reputable
training school to minimse the chances of a wrong control
input denting the machine and your pride. Typically, this
will involve about 5 hours of dual flying with an instructor,
and perhaps 1–2 hours of solo consolidation. Recently,
Pegasus Flight Training has successfully converted to
weight-shift an A.T.P.L. with 9,000 hours, an ex-Sunderland
and Shackleton skipper, a professional navigator and several
P.P.L. As. They all reported that they thoroughly enjoyed
back-to-basics flying and some went on to purchase
machines.

The first thing you'll notice when you climb aboard is that
the seating position is decidedly cosy, and the instrumenta-
tion is basic. Typically, you will be confronted by an airspeed
indicator (in m.p.h.), a compass, an altimeter, and usually a
vertical speed indicator and rev counter/cylinder head
temperature gauge. There are two throttles: a foot throttle on
the front forks and a hand throttle on the seat frame. The
reason for this soon becomes obvious. When taxying, taking

The CFM Shadow (above) is a microlight of British origin that has conventional flying controls, while the Pegasus type (below) is controlled by weightshift

off and landing you will need both hands on the control bar, so you use the foot throttle. When cruising, you set the hand throttle to the desired r.p.m. The nose wheel steering operates like a land yacht, so push left, go right. The quickest way to acclimatise is to spend some time taxying without the wing attached and it soon becomes natural. Next try taxying whilst keeping the wings level. If there is a crosswind, dip the windward wing slightly to prevent the wind getting underneath. In this way you can taxi in quite strong winds.

In practice, you will then do the upper air exercises with your instructor. After the pre-flight, pre-start and pre-take-off checks, you will notice that you have to make sure that the wings are level before you start the take-off roll. In a conventional aircraft, there is of course no choice. Acceleration is rapid and the take-off roll is very short. Rotate the nose upwards (push the control bar away from you), and as soon as the wheels leave the ground, relax the pressure on the bar and let it return to the neutral position. Count to two, speed up to 50 m.p.h. until you reach 200 feet, then slow to 40 m.p.h. which is best climbing speed. Because of their light weight, these aircraft are more affected by turbulence, so positive control inputs are necessary nearer the ground.

Once in the air you will have time to relax. Your touch on the control bar should be light but positive; most beginners overcontrol. You'll be surprised how stable the aircraft is. Trim speed is usually 50–55 m.p.h. and pitch pressure is light. Roll is generally heavier, although it lightens considerably at speed. With regard to control reversals forget about the stick but think in terms of moving yourself in the direction you wish to follow. Move forwards (bar in) the nose comes down. Move left, the left wing comes down. Practise roll whilst driving by putting both hands on the bottom of the steering wheel and you will soon get the idea.

Turns should be well co-ordinated: move left, wait until the wing comes down to the desired angle of bank, centralise on the bar and at moderate bank angles the aircraft will fly a perfect circle. At higher bank angles, you will need to raise the nose slightly, and increase power slightly. Remember you are not using a stick, and because the mechanics of the wing dictate that yaw is a secondary effect of roll, thrashing about on the rudder bar will have no effect.

As for the rest, the principles are all the same; it is merely the method of achieving them which is different. Stalls are considerably more gentle than on conventional aircraft, with plenty of advance warning. Height loss on a full stall can be as little as 50 feet when properly controlled. Landing takes the most practice, but it is very satisfying when well done. A glide approach is the safest. Approach at 50 m.p.h., power off, wings level and keep roll control movements to a minimum to prevent oscillation on finals. Raise the nose slightly at 15 feet. Aim to round out at 2 feet. Control movements in both roll and pitch will of course get progressively larger as the speed reduces, so your final pitch movement will be bar fully forward, usually at about 30 m.p.h. After landing, pull the nose down to prevent ballooning and to assist braking.

As you will have learned to fly aircraft that will provide economical flying with a minimum of hassle, you can fly out of farmers' fields, so air traffic clearance is unnecessary. You can pack the aircraft away in half an hour, so expensive hangarage is a thing of the past. You can fly with or without radio. Fuel and maintenance costs are very low and engine reliability is good. Above all, you will discover that this basic form of aviation is fun.

You may have noticed a certain anomaly in the licensing system. With a Group A P.P.L. you are not permitted to fly a self-launching motor glider (which has conventional flying controls) without obtaining an additional (S.L.M.G.) endorsement. However, you may fly a weight-shift microlight, with its control movements that are the reverse of those to which you are accustomed, without further qualifications. Take care, though, not to let either of these situations dictate your next move, as a rating for an S.L.M.G. is easy enough to obtain and you would be foolish to fly weight-shift without guidance just because this is permitted by law. Either style of flight is available to anyone who seeks it, so try whichever appeals, or both.

Floatplanes, gyroplanes, helicopters

Another activity that may be available is the chance to fly a floatplane. There is much to learn about operating an aeroplane from, to and on water, with many attendant ground support skills to acquire; unfortunately very few facilities exist in this country, but if the opportunity arises, take it. I have tried it only once, but I enjoyed every minute.

Flying from water has its own appeal and calls for its own skills. Here is a Piper Cub on floats.

I have omitted details of the forms of aviation that are not directly related to aeroplane piloting skills, such as parachuting or ballooning, but these, too, may attract your interest and each offers its own brand of airborne experience. Helicopters, though, warrant more of a mention, for with your existing P.P.L. you will be granted a reduction of 10 hours on the 40 required for the P.P.L.(H), but the prices are high and a three-figure hourly rate for tuition or hire may be a deterrent for most people. Finally, there is a licence for pilots why fly gyroplanes, but nationally the number is barely into double figures.

There are almost endless pleasures if you take the trouble to seek and find them, but always remember to take every precaution with regard to safety (see Appendix 2).

8
Your Flying Future

For a short time after qualifying for your pilot's licence you are most likely to remain with the flying centre where you trained. If you intend only to fly occasionally, you may choose to stay with that organisation indefinitely. There are certain advantages in doing so; you will be confident of flying an aeroplane with a Certificate of Airworthiness in the Transport category; you will have access to a flying instructor if you wish to obtain higher qualifications, or if you need an occasional check-out or brush-up; there will be a positive booking system to enable you to reserve an aeroplane in advance; and you will maintain contact both socially and technically with other people who have similar interests.

Unfortunately, the training system is such that most instructors are fully occupied teaching the regular flow of new students, or dealing with those qualified pilots who enrol on advanced courses. You may be one of the latter, but if not and you wish to be given a check flight to ensure that your standards, practices and procedures are not slipping too seriously, then be certain to ask. Most probably the organisation will insist that you fly with an instructor at periodic intervals, particularly when your licence is new and your experience is limited, or if you have not flown for a while. If you need more help, advice and guidance to keep you in good shape, then by staying with the training organisation that facility will be available. Remember though that the economics of a flying school or club are very tight, with very small margins, and the instructors' time is valuable and you must not resent being asked to pay extra for dual when compared with the normal hire rate for the aircraft.

Apart from any formal arrangement to fly with an instructor, you can pick up a growing knowledge of aviation by associating with the other pilots. There are those around who have been flying for longer than you have and they may be pleased to offer free guidance based on their experiences, while other pilots who have similar flying backgrounds to yours may be interesting to listen to. Talking about flying can be both entertaining and useful. There is much to gain now in discussing problems about navigation, crosswinds, radio aids, engine handling, or airmanship as there was when you were a student, but now you will be building extra knowledge from a higher base. It all helps to make you a better and more competent pilot. Where flying is concerned, no one stops learning and anyone who feels that his knowledge is sufficient would do well to reconsider the wisdom of that view, or take up a different pastime. The motto of the General Aviation Safety Committee, about which I will mention more a little later, is 'Safety Through Knowledge'.

It is not essential to take more courses or obtain further qualifications. Even if you wish to be a 'Summer Sunday' pilot and not venture very far from home, you will gain experience and knowledge from discussion, observation and, of course, from your own experience of flying. You must decide on the best course of action to suit your own circumstances. Time, money, family responsibilities and your reasons for wanting to fly must all be considered. There is no harm in treating the P.P.L as your sole aim, with no desire or intention to add any further ratings, but once you have gone to the lengths of obtaining that licence, no doubt you will wish to put it to work rather than to waste it.

The Cessna 182 Skylane is unusual among private single-engine aircraft in having a retractable undercarriage

Hiring aircraft

Apart from aeroplanes available from your training centre, machines may be hired from organisations that deal solely with licensed pilots. Aircraft may be offered 'dry' or 'wet', by the hour, the day, the weekend or even the week. However, before committing yourself to doing business with a strange, unknown company, it is advisable to check its credentials. Make sure that the aeroplane is in the Transport category (which is legally essential if you are paying money for it), find out what type and extent of insurance cover exists and whether the published charges are all-inclusive, or whether there are hidden extras in the small print.

Co-ownership Flying Groups

If you are happy with a specific type of aircraft and wish to do a reasonable amount of flying without paying the full commercial rates of the hiring companies, you should consider joining a co-ownership group. There are hundreds of these around Britain and I doubt if any general aviation aerodrome is without one or more among its regular residents. These organisations are run on a voluntary basis, with some members undertaking specific tasks. They vary enormously; in one case an aeroplane may be owned and operated by only three or four people; in another, the group may have twenty or more members and be ready to take on another at any time. Obviously, the larger the membership the smaller the sum you will be required to pay as your entry share, but equally the more people who share one machine the greater the competition for its use — especially at peak times.

There is little point in joining any group if you intend or, for one reason or another, are able to fly only the minimum of hours to keep your licence valid, as the costs will be higher than hiring commercially. You will need to pay a sum on entry to buy your share in the aeroplane and then you will be required to pay a fixed monthly or quarterly charge to cover overheads such as insurance, hangarage, routine maintenance and depreciation. You will also need to cover direct operating costs for any flying you undertake. The break-even point must depend on all these factors, but when you know what the expenses will be and how many hours you hope to fly in a year, you will be able to calculate whether there is any economic advantage for you in this arrangement. Cost, of course, is not the only subject to consider. You must be satisfied that the aircraft type operated by the group will satisfy your needs in all respects. If you have members of the family who may wish to fly with you, you will be unpopular if you settle for a two-seater, however attractive this may seem to you as a machine to fly. Once you are in the group and faced with regular outgoings, you will wish to gain maximum return by using the aeroplane as much as possible. You may or may not want radio aids but, if not, there is little point in committing yourself to the capital cost and subsequent running expenses of expensive equipment which you will not use. Ask yourself various questions about the aeroplane such as whether it is aerobatic. This may not be important unless you have the urge to develop your flying skills in the field of pure flight. Is it a type for which engine and airframe spares are readily available? Is the machine maintained professionally, by a reputable and reliable orga-nisation, or will your chances of getting in the air when you wish to do so, depend on a member of the group who may or may not be available? If the latter applies, this is not necessarily bad, for the work may be carried out by an engineer who has a pilot's licence and who is rewarded in flying time. This is less expensive than paying money to a company and results in cheaper flying for all members.

Personalities are important in the successful operation of a group, for it is a form of co-operative and every member must realise his responsibilities to the others. If someone operates a tight administrative system, especially regarding bookings for the aeroplane, then there should not be any problem. With a total dependence on voluntary effort, there can be no room for anyone who is inconsiderate. Flight records should be maintained and be readily accessible, particularly with regard to the booking system, so that at popular periods all concerned can have their allotted times in the air. One person can ruin a day for all the others by taking the aircraft away for a long time and not notifying anyone about where he has gone, or when he intends to return. There are few greater frustrations than booking the machine, waking to a fine, bright day, looking forward to giving a flight to a friend and arriving at the aerodrome only to see the aeroplane taking-off and disappearing from view at the time you had planned to fly. In a well-regulated group this should not happen.

If you are able to fly at times when most people are at work, then a group may offer the ideal solution. In some cases the aeroplane may be booked only for hourly sessions at weekends, with wholeday reservations permissible from Mondays to Fridays. If there is no other demand for the machine when you want it, you may be able to fly to a destination and leave it there for several hours without any financial penalty for waiting time. This is a bonus that not many schools or clubs are able to offer, but it makes a day out by air a practical reality at a reasonable cost. The other main point to consider is insurance (see Chapter 9), as this has special significance in relation to group operations.

If you cannot find a group which suits you, you may wish to consider forming one yourself. You should have little difficulty in finding other pilots who are willing to join you in your venture. A considerable amount of work is involved however, for not only must you have access to the right aeroplane and appropriate people with whom to share, but you will need to ensure that all the related tasks are dealt with efficiently. A chairman, secretary, treasurer, bookings person and engineer are the starting points. Then you must be sure that your home aerodrome (or, if not, another base) will accept the aeroplane and the arrangement on mutually agreed terms, including permission to operate at any sensible time on any day. The group will need to be formally constituted with separate membership and flying rules. It may also be advisable to form the organisation into a company limited by guarantee for added protection. The eventual rewards can be well worth the effort, but only if those who join you are as determined as you to make it a success. A guideline paper has been produced by the Aircraft Owners and Pilots Association.

Private aircraft ownership

This is expensive but provides the only certain way to ensure that your aeroplane is available whenever you want it. The price to pay for this exclusive privilege includes initial purchase (and no worthwhile machine is cheap to buy), hangarage or parking, maintenance, insurance, depreciation and all running costs. If you are likely to need to fly on business at short notice, then this may provide your answer. To be able to travel about anywhere at virtually any time, you will need some comprehensive avionics (radio equipment), and you will be unable to put this to full use unless your own experience and training can match it. If there is one way in which newcomers to flying have genuine cause to be frustrated, it is when they start with the idea that a brand new P.P.L. will open the gate to everywhere at all times. There are many ways in which you can use and enjoy your licence, but serious business travel to meet tight deadlines cannot be one. Please note that total dependence on your own aeroplane and your own skills and abilities to get you to an important meeting is something that must wait until you are more qualified.

The total costs of personal ownership may be more than you anticipate and almost certainly higher than those quoted by any zealous salesman. Whilst you will know the precise purchase price, the likely aerodrome charges and the insurance for at least a year ahead, servicing figures are almost always underestimated. Most quoted prices are based on routine inspections and make little if any allowances for components that fail or wear out prematurely. All items used in aircraft must comply with standards set by the Airworthiness Division of the Civil Aviation Authority, and this requirement can put the price of a simple bolt to a figure four times the amount payable on the household market. So consider the value of an engine if you should need one.

There are ways of reducing the financial shock. You may be able to share your aircraft with one other person as a partner. Ideally one of you may wish to fly mainly at weekends and the other during the working week, in which case the machine's usage can be well-balanced. In such a case, each of you has virtually all the advantages of sole ownership, but at half the total cost. Another possibility is to operate the aircraft as part of a trading company or even form the aeroplane and its operation into a company of its own. If capital outlay is a drawback but regular subsequent outgoings are acceptable, hire purchase or straightforward leasing are alternatives. There is no shortage of organisations eager to have your custom in such an arrangement.

Building your own aeroplane

Another way of owning an aeroplane is to build one yourself. If this sounds a distant dream, let me surprise you by saying that several hundred light aircraft are under construction by amateur builders at any one time. Most of these are of fairly basic structural design, but dozens of types are suitable for the purpose and there may be one to suit you. The main problem is not so much the monetary cost, but the amount of time that you are able and willing to devote to the task and the resources at your disposal. You need a workshop and you require practical woodworking or engineering skills, but ample help is available so long as you can provide and maintain the driving force to keep the project on the move. The design must be approved and the work must be checked at intervals by an inspector from the Popular Flying Association, which has delegated authority from the Civil Aviation Authority to oversee home-building in Britain.

Normally a self-made aeroplane takes to the air with a Permit to Fly instead of a full Certificate of Airworthiness, but for purely private purposes this is not restrictive. Before embarking on such a venture, though, consider all the implications. Will this have an adverse effect on your family and household? Are you prepared to devote several hours each week without fail? Will you be happy with the chosen type as the end product? Can you wait a few years and still afford both the time and the money to keep your licence valid while you are building your new machine? If you are not deterred by these rather deep-hitting questions, then you and a home-built aeroplane may get along well together. Ultimately, you will have your own machine, made with your own hands, and will be able to show it proudly to other pilots and at specialist rallies. The relatively modest total cost will have been spread over as many years as you take to complete the job.

Keeping up to date

If you fly with a club or group you will have opportunities to meet many other people with similar interests, but the light side of the general aviation movement spreads far afield and you have much to gain by keeping in touch on a wider basis. There are several aviation journals to read. Some cover aviation as a whole, extending beyond our type of flying to jumbos, military operations and spaceflight, while others specialise in private aviation, historic aircraft or the wishes of the aeroplane enthusiast or aeromodeller.

There are single- and two-seat versions of the Pitts Special aerobatic biplanes

It is very easy to become parochial in one's outlook on aviation and aeroplanes, but you can avoid this by keeping in close contact with what goes on. As a private pilot or aircraft owner the Aircraft Owners' and Pilots' Association has a place awaiting you, while if you start or run a co-ownership group you can enrol in corporate membership. If you intend to build your own aeroplane or are specially interested in ultra-light machines, the Popular Flying Association would be a more appropriate organisation. If you should become an owner of, or actively involved in flying an historic aeroplane, the Vintage Aircraft Club runs events at which you will meet others with similar interests. These organisations are well and truly embroiled in the activities to which they relate and you will gain much from the usually modest subscription which you will be asked to pay (see Chapter 10).

Private flying offers almost endless possibilites and with a little thought about what you would like to do and then setting your mind on doing it, there is neither need nor excuse for frustration or boredom.

9
Insurance

Flying is remarkably safe. Statistically motoring is not as safe yet, despite the figures, some insurers are guilty of increasing their rates for people who they consider are foolhardy enough to take their lives into the air. Even if all motorists operate strictly within the terms of the law (and many fail to do so) the maximum permitted speed of 70 m.p.h. means that two cars meeting head-on will have a joint closing speed of 140 m.p.h. Few light aeroplanes are likely to hit the ground at much more than about a third of that figure and whilst faster speeds can apply in mid-air collision, the likelihood is remote. In our cars we travel in opposing directions with only a few feet between us, but in the air we take avoiding action as soon as we see another aircraft that is even marginally likely to become too close for comfort. In airspace that is controlled, others help us to ensure that such an incident does not occur.

You may be surprised to know that there is no compulsion for anyone to have any insurance cover for his aircraft, for himself, or for his passengers, or against third party risks. Although anyone who fails to buy any protection is acting irresponsibly, this freedom creates a problem for the person who intends to act sensibly but who may make one minor slip. In the case of a car, for which third party insurance is mandatory, the insuring company cannot escape from responsibility through the owner's or driver's forgetfulness. All motor policies must state that cover is in force so long as the driver holds, or has held, and is not disqualified from holding a licence. In short, if the licence has expired, but the cover has not, the protection remains. This is not the case with aviation insurance. As there is no compulsion for the owner, operator or pilot to have any cover, there is no compulsion for the insurer to provide it.

You have a pilot's licence on which the medical and experience elements must be maintained. If either should be out of date, even by one day, you are unlicensed and an insurer can back out from what most of us say is a moral responsibility for it is not a legal one. If you have obtained an I.M.C. Rating but there is an incident one day after that rating has expired when you are flying in conditions that call for that qualification, you have no protection even though your licence is valid. For example, if your aeroplane has a Certificate of Airworthiness in the private category and you are carrying a passenger or a parcel, for which some reward has been paid or offered, and something goes wrong your insurance will not cover the situation. A comparable situation applies, of course, if you have a P.P.L. and you are carrying out a similar operation, even if the machine is correctly certificated. In brief, if any one item of the operation is not wholly within the law, the insurance company is likely to repudiate any claim. In the event of a genuine error, some of the better organisations may offer ex-gratia settlement, but it is unsafe to take risks on the grounds that this will be the case.

While all this may sound worrying, it is not serious enough to cause concern if you take steps to keep your aviation affairs in order. One way is to make suitable notes in key places, such as slipping a piece of paper in your flying logbook stating when various things expire. Then, each time you record a flight, you will see what is needed in the way of renewals. It is essential to operate wholly within the law in relation to the limitations of your licence and the airworthiness of the aeroplane.

Personal accident policy

Insurance affects everyone who flies and not just aircraft owners. If you have a personal accident policy it may exclude flying. Check to see if it does. If so, you can contact your broker to see the extent to which the premium would be increased if you add the relevant cover, or you can join a scheme provided exclusively for private pilots. One example of cover available at very reasonable rates is the A.O.P.A. Wings Scheme, which is open to all members of the Aircraft

Owners' and Pilots' Association. This may be more economical than extending a normal policy with a company unfamiliar with aviation. However, you will be wise to make comparisons.

Hull cover

If you are an owner or even if you have a small share in a group-owned machine, you will be wise to obtain hull cover at a realistic value. Failing this, you will lose badly if the aeroplane is damaged in an accident. As a sole owner you may consider the risk worthwhile if no one else flies the aircraft but, in the case of collective ownership, you will lose money when someone else damages the aeroplane. Most groups have sensible cover, but before you join one you should insist on knowing the details. An increasingly popular scheme among light aircraft owners is the very competitive AOPAPLAN, which is exclusive to members of the association. Most hull policies have compulsory excess figures but, fortunately for very little cost, you can buy separate cover.

Third party cover

The most important cover is the protection against claims by third parties. Many owners grossly under-insure their interests. It is difficult to be sure how much cover you will need, so it is sensible to insure for as much as you can afford. For instance, if your house, domestic and business interests are collectively worth, say, £150,000 and you have cover for £2 million, you cannot be accused of being irresponsible. If you are a millionaire and have an aeroplane with only £100,000 third party protection, someone may have no qualms about pressing for more than the full value of your possessions. As a rough guide, for the average light aeroplane carrying out normal operations, a sum of £1m is a sound *minimum* figure upon which to work.

Special third party cover

There are several other forms of cover that are available and in some cases are essential. Special third party protection to the value of £5m is required by the Ministry of Defence for anyone landing at military airfields, many of which are available for use by private aircraft. If you intend to use these bases regularly, you can purchase a special indemnity policy valid for a year, but in the case of an occasional landing at a Service airfield a new facility provides one-off cover by payment of an appropriate sum on top of the basic landing fee. A voluntary but advisable form of cover is for passenger liability, which provides protection against claims from occupants of the aeroplane that you are flying.

If you fly sensibly, you will fly safely, but however careful you may be, you must not convince yourself or be persuaded that nothing can happen to you. Statistically, you are likely to fly for year after year without causing or receiving so much as a scratch, but when, very occasionally, something does go amiss, the size of the claim may be quite large.

Take the trouble to understand the insurance that you are buying and satisfy yourself that you have adequate cover. For example, if you have an aeroplane with a replacement value of £25,000 and you insure it for only half that sum, you may find that a relatively minor accident (such as an undercarriage collapse, bending the propeller, shock-loading the engine and scraping the underside) will put you into a financially embarrassing position. Repairs may cost about £10,000, the insurers elect to declare the aircraft a total loss (and the decision is theirs, not yours) and they will pay you £12,500 less any excess. The aircraft is theirs and they sell it for at least the insured value, therefore recovering their outgoings. But you have no aeroplane and only half the money with which to buy a replacement. Under-valuing your possessions can be a false economy. Also, you should take care to complete the insurance proposal form accurately, as the information that you put on it becomes the basis of the contract. If you state that the machine is to be used for private and business purposes and then you indulge in aerial photography or carrying passengers for hire or reward, the whole agreement will be invalidated. If you intend to allow your machine to be used by a flying club, this must be declared; and then, of course, it must be on a Transport category C. of A. There are many other possible examples, but above all remember that it pays to be honest.

Insurance costs money and takes both time and thought to arrange effectively but, with proper protection, you have nothing to fear in the way of claims made against you or your estate.

10
Behind the Daily Scene

Civil Aviation Authority

All activities relating to civil aviation in the U.K. are subject to requirements laid down by the Civil Aviation Authority (C.A.A.). In turn, the authority owes allegiance to the Department of Transport (D.Tp.), which itself is responsible to Parliament. The C.A.A. has many branches, but has two main divisions: one dealing with operations and the other with airworthiness. In earlier years the latter task was handled by a separate organisation known as the Air Registration Board.

Within the operations side of the C.A.A., the sections dealing with flight crew licensing, aerodromes, airspace and air traffic control are of main concern to those who fly. The authority operates on a consultative basis with all the organisations that represent the various sectors within the total aviation framework. When we consider international airlines, domestic airlines, commuter carriers, air taxi operators, charter companies, crop-sprayers, banner towers, flying schools and clubs, private pilots, gliding and soaring fraternity, parachutists, microlight fliers, those who hang-glide, parascenders, fliers of balloons and the occasional airship, with the added and diverse needs of military aviation by the Royal Navy, the Army and the Royal Air Force, we have a vast network of needs that are hard to meet to the satisfaction of all.

Representative organisations

Many private pilots complain that they do not receive enough attention and certainly light aviation must work hard to make itself felt in its search for effective action. It is only through the various representative organisations that each section of the aviation community can press its case. In return the associations depend entirely on those who fly to provide essential support.

Among the problems to be resolved on a continuing basis are availability and sharing of airspace; availability of airports and aerodromes, with facilities geared to the needs of the various categories of users; pilots' licences, ratings and endorsements; availability of fuel supplies, of the right grades in the right places and at the times needed; meteorological services where and when required; customs and immigration; en route and terminal facilities (in the form of various types of radio navigation aids); a broad range of matters relating to airworthiness, covering aspects relating to airframes, engines, propellers, instruments, radio and ancillary items; and, of course, the costs of all these and the way in which they are passed on.

The major organisation that handles matters on behalf of the lighter sector of general aviation is the Aircraft Owners' and Pilots' Association of the United Kingdom (A.O.P.A. U.K.). This is part of the worldwide International A.O.P.A., which operates in thirty-three countries and has a total membership of nearly 350,000 pilots. It is the world's largest general aviation organisation. Unfortunately, for a number of reasons, the scale of the operation in the U.K. is relatively small with only 6,850 aeroplanes on the British civil register, 6,000 of which are in the general aviation category, making it the largest sector. However, the financial weight lies mainly with the minority, such as the airlines and tour operators, and the light aircraft user needs to plan his case carefully if his input is to be heard and accepted. This is why the future freedom of private pilots depends on the strength of the associations which exist to support their cause.

An organisation with an important role in the world of light aviation is the Popular Flying Association. This deals with all matters relating to home-built aircraft and has delegated authority from the C.A.A. to carry out design approval, inspections at various stages of construction and recommendations for the issue and renewal of permits to fly. The association's activities go beyond this, though, with membership groups, or struts as they are called, spread over Britain. Each year, the P.F.A. runs the largest private aircraft rally on the U.K. aviation calendar. Other bodies, such as the

British Gliding Association, the British Microlight Aircraft Association, the British Aerobatic Association, British Women Pilot's Association and the Vintage Aircraft Club have their own specific aims and activities.

Frequently, these various organisations that make up the total aviation scene operate together. You may wonder, therefore, why there are so many separate bodies and why they cannot be rolled into one. The reason is that each has its own particular problems with which to deal, and we cannot expect, for example, the microlight people to devote time, energy, money and attention to a proposed change in the requirements for operating helicopters in instrument flight conditions! However, there is some overlap on many subjects. For example, a proposal for a change in the renewal requirements for private pilots' licences would be of concern to the Aircraft Owners' and Pilots' Association, the Popular Flying Association and, on behalf of its tug pilots, the British Gliding Association.

Because of the range of subjects covering U.K. aviation, several consultative committees exist to allow open discussion between the authorities and the representative bodies. One of the largest of these is the National Air Traffic Management Advisory Committee. This is administered by the National Air Traffic Service, which itself is a composite body drawn from the Civil Aviation Authority and the Ministry of Defence. Nearly seventy people might be present at such a meeting, which takes a whole day. Not all agenda items affect every member, but the opportunity for all opinions to be heard and all views to be expressed has considerable value. When one organisation submitted a proposal for a change in the rules for visual flight, naturally this aroused the active involvement of both A.O.P.A. and the P.F.A. Unexpectedly, the representative of the smaller independent airlines held similar views to those of the private flying fraternity. Any alteration would have affected the flights carried out on the scheduled services between the various Scottish islands where much of the flying time requires visual contact with the ground.

A much smaller committee, performing a very different

function, is the C.A.A.'s Standing Advisory Committee on Private Pilot Licensing. Here the authority deals directly with the bodies actively concerned with the training of pilots and their subsequent rights and privileges. Situations rarely stand still and always there are proposals for changes; surprisingly, ideas (or even plans for the imposition of added restrictions) do not necessarily originate from the C.A.A. Sometimes they come from within a sector of the flying movement, where one group seeks to affect the freedom or expenses of another. All such ideas must be considered by the Authority, and this committee provides the forum at which opposing views are discussed.

There are numerous other working groups offering contact between the Authority and those who must make aviation work in the field but liaison, discussion and even argument, are not restricted to the time spent in formally constituted committees. Regular correspondence and frequent meetings between individuals ensure that all subjects and problems are aired continuously. Only one or two people may attend a meeting with a particular department within the Authority, or with Customs, or with the fuel companies, yet many others may need to know the outcome. The A.O.P.A., for example, under the main Board and an Executive Committee, has a Corporate Committee (for flying training organisations), an Instructors Committee, an Owners' Committee and a Pilots' Committee, each one of which has a collective duty to attend to the needs and interests of its own particular section of aviation activity. Similarly, the Popular Flying Association has an active and permanent working relationship with the C.A.A. Airworthiness Division regarding the wide range of aircraft (some of which are one-off examples) operating under the Permit-to-Fly system. In turn the Association must keep close contact with its team of inspectors who are spread all over the U.K.

International Civil Aviation

So far I have dealt only with subjects that originate and are handled entirely within the U.K.; however the International

Civil Aviation Organisation provides criteria for many matters that affect us all. For example, the results of worldwide inputs and deliberations at I.C.A.O. may result in an increase in the minimum number of hours to be flown before a pilot can qualify for a P.P.L. A nation may 'file a difference', but only if the figures put forward exceed those minima agreed by I.C.A.O. Radio frequency allocations, too, have an international element, with certain bands allotted to specific types of use. Whilst within the agreed bands, individual frequencies are allocated to specific sites on an internal basis, any shortage of band space may result in difficulties at local levels. Many private aircraft have 360-channel V.H.F. radio sets and these can operate only on frequencies with 50 kiloHertz spacing; but a facility needed by those users may be issued with a frequency to a tighter spread of only 25 kHz. This requires aircraft using it to have more modern and more expensive sets covering 720 channels. This is where the associations come in again and certainly A.O.P.A. can claim a recent but important win in just such an instance, affecting a much-needed radar facility used extensively by light aircraft.

The importance of personal involvement

The main point that I wish to emphasise is the importance of the various representative organisations. There is a need for more people to become actively involved beyond the confines of the cockpit, the club house or the crew room. Not every private pilot can expect to be in a position of direct contact with the policy-making levels of the C.A.A., but every person who is concerned for the future of flying can support the system by joining the association appropriate to his interests. By staying outside the network you are increasing the relative strength of the opposition and encouraging such action against the movement in which you are interested. Private flying has an enormous amount to offer and needs the support of its members.

Appendix 1

Medical requirements for Private Pilots

by A. H. Roscoe M.D., D.Av. Med., F.R.Ae.S. Chief Medical Officer, Britannia Airways.

Any practising pilot must have a valid licence containing a current certificate of medical fitness issued by an Authorised Medical Examiner (A.M.E.) appointed by the C.A.A. U.K. Medical Standards are based on those recommended by the International Civil Aviation Organisation (I.C.A.O.) in Annex I – *Personnel Licensing*.

A professional pilot requires a Class I Medical Certificate but a private pilot requires only a Class III certificate, with the exception of full and assistant instructors who now require recently re-introduced Class II medical certificates.

It is unusual for a pilot under the age of 50 to lose his licence on medical grounds; there have been only 15 failures over a period of 10 years. As a result of the low incidences of medical problems in this age group, the intervals between medical examinations have recently been extended. The periods of validity of Class III medical certificates are:

Pilots under 40   – 5 years
Pilots aged 40–50 – 2 years
Pilots aged 50–70 – 1 year
Pilots over 70   – 6 months

Because of the increased vulnerability to coronary heart disease in middle age (90% of medical failure in pilots over 50 are due to cardio-vascular disease) resting electrocardiograms (E.E.G.) are now required more frequently:

Pilots aged 40–50 – every 4 years
Pilots aged 50–60 – every 2 years
Pilots aged 60–70 – annually
Pilots over 70   – every 6 months

About half the number of flying instructors and assistant flying instructors currently fly on Private Pilots' Licences. In view of the greater amount of flying carried out by instructors it is now necessary for them to have Class II medical certificates, which involves a baseline E.C.G. being carried out at the first medical examination. X-ray examination of the chest is not now required unless there are clinical indications. Doubtful or borderline cases are normally referred to the Medical Branch of the C.A.A. for assessment by the Authority's Medical Officers.

A pilot who flies only microlight aircraft is exempt from the full P.P.L. medical requirements. A declaration of health, signed by the person concerned and counter-signed by his or her Medical Practitioner, is sufficient.

As mentioned earlier, 90% of medical failures are due to cardio-vascular disease, such as high blood pressure and coronary heart disease. Undoubtedly, probability of losing one's licence for these reasons can be reduced considerably by modifying one's life style. For example, smoking increases the likelihood of cardio-vascular disease significantly, the chance of developing high blood pressure is increased by being overweight, and a diet high in animal fats and cholesterol increases the likelihood of heart disease. Regular physical exercise not only reduces the chance of cardio-vascular disease but also improves your performance as a pilot by making you that much 'sharper'.

Just as you have an interest in the mechanical state of your aeroplane — so you should have an interest in maintaining a reasonable state of health.

Appendix 2

Safety: A Combination of Learning, Experience and Attitude of Mind

by John Ward MBE Chairman and Secretary of The General Aviation Safety Committee

There is an often-used saying in aviation flight safety circles to the effect that there is nothing inherently unsafe about flying, but it is an activity that is terribly unforgiving of any human error, carelessness or neglect. Put another way, flying accidents are caused by people and, to judge by the twenty years experience of the U.K. General Aviation Safety Committee (usually referred to as GASCo), the person usually responsible is the pilot. In fact, in the great majority of general aviation accidents the cause is invariably some error or omission on the part of the pilot. There have been very few flying accidents in which the pilot was not involved in any way.

It follows that, for a flight to be conducted without injury or hurt to anyone, there are three essential requirements for the pilot. First he must have been properly trained and, in this connection, getting a licence is only a small, albeit important part of the training of a pilot. Indeed, on initial issue a pilot's licence really is little more than a licence to learn. For it is probably more true of aviation than most other human activities that one never 'knows it all'; and normally the more flying experience that a pilot has, the more he realises how much there is still to learn. As one 20,000 hour veteran once said, 'I may not have done as much flying as some pilots, but I have now done just enough to realise how little I know about flying'.

The second requirement is for the pilot to be 'current'; that is, he must be up to date in every aspect he is likely to meet during the flight. That means, of course, not only in respect of flying skills and handling of the controls as well as recent practice in emergency procedures and drills, but also such things as changes in the rules and regulations, frequencies when appropriate, and location of controlled, danger, restricted and prohibited airspace. No matter how clever he may have proved himself to have been during his general flying test and ground examinations, skills and knowledge do degenerate with the passage of time, sometimes even if you do fly every day, and have to be refreshed and polished to retain the bright edge that they had on graduation day. A high level of both skill and knowledge is not only an important element for success in an unexpected situation, but it also ensures efficiency and economy in every sense of the word during perfectly uneventful operations.

The final and possibly most important attribute, but probably the most difficult to acquire, is the pilot's attitude of mind towards flying. To some extent the right approach to aviation can be learned during initial training, and the influence of a flying instructor can be a vitally important factor in the early stages. If the instructor's approach is 'do as I say and not as I do' and he then indulges in some low aerobatics over a girl friend's home, this is a recipe for disaster, not so much for him as for his student. But no matter how good an instructor may be and how well he trains the fledgelings in his temporary care, a pilot's personal characteristics will be his saviour or downfall in a simple emergency situation, whether of his own making or not, and this applies even before he leaves the careful supervision of his instructor.

Aviation really is terribly sensitive to human behaviour. The pilot who plans meticulously, practises often and studies carefully will *appear* to take risks and 'get away with it', whereas he is really operating quite safely. On the other hand, however, anger, haste, pride, frustration, exhibitionism, overconfidence, laziness, distraction, boredom, complacency, anxiety, insecurity, you name it and it will have been given as the reason why a pilot, even a highly qualified and experienced one, became involved in a flying accident. However, if these shortcomings can be recognised by the individual aviator and a conscious effort made to eliminate or at least to control them when they are recognised in his own behaviour, the result will be not only a safe operation but a thrilling and very satisfying one too.

(The General Aviation Safety Committee publishes the quarterly Flight Safety Bulletin. This is recommended reading for all who fly.)

Appendix 3

Circular sent to Private Pilots
by The Flight Crew Licensing Department of the Civil Aviation Authority.

Flight Crew Licensing 3
Room 344

Maintaining the validity of a Private Pilot's Licence

As the proud holder of a Private Pilot's Licence you will now wish to enjoy to the full the privileges of the licence and the various ratings for which you have qualified, or may qualify for in the future. In particular, you will wish to know what you must do to maintain the validity of the licence and the aircraft ratings included in the licence.

Before you may exercise the privileges of your P.P.L. you must hold a current medical certificate, issued by an authorised medical examiner (A.M.E.), by a C.A.A. medical officer, or, in the case of a P.P.L. (Microlights), a Form 150/AB signed by your own medical practitioner. The validity period of a medical certificate depends on the class of medical certificate issued and your age. The various validity periods are included in the medical certificate, to which you should refer.

To maintain the validity of the aircraft rating(s) included in your licence you must obtain at intervals of 13 months either a Certificate of Experience (C. of E.) or a Certificate of Test (C. of T.). The C. of E. or C. of T. must be stamped in your personal flying logbook and be signed by a person authorised by the C.A.A. to sign Cs. of E. or one authorised to carry out flight tests for a C. of T.

To qualify for a C. of E. you must show evidence of having gained 5 hours flying experience in the group(s) of aircraft to which the C. of E. refers in the 13 months immediately preceding the date of signing of the C. of E. These 5 hours may include not more than 2 hours of dual instruction, but the remaining 3 hours must be as unsupervised pilot-in-command. Also, you must have made at least one flight in an aircraft representative of each of the Groups you wish to fly, or the specific type in the case of Group C or helicopters.

If you do not have sufficient flying experience to qualify for a C. of E., then you must undertake a flight test with a P.P.L. (X) examiner or, in the case of a Group C or a helicopter with a Type Rating examiner (T.R.E.). The content of the test will depend on the circumstances, but provided you have flown as pilot-in-command within the *four years* since the date of your last C. of E. or C. of T. then the P.P.L (X) examiner will be able to advise you of the test and training requirements. If more than four years have elapsed, then you must write to the C.A.A. (FCL3) for an assessment of the training and test requirements. Please remember to include your personal flying logbook and any other pilot licences you may hold when requesting such an assessment.

You should understand that to fly without a valid medical certificate or outside the validity of any C. of E. or C. of T. is a breach of the legislation and could lead to prosecution.

Enjoy your flying and happy landings!

Appendix 4

General aviation organisations and official controlling bodies

The organisations listed below can provide authoritative information on specific general aviation activities in the United Kingdom

Aerodrome Owners Association (AOA) 18 Orchard Street, Bristol, Avon BS1 5DX. Tel: (0272) 292480. Represents interests of U.K. aerodrome owners.

The Air Education and Recreation Organisation (AERO) The Teachers Centre, 118 Upper Chobham Road, Camberley, Surrey. Tel: (0276) 61951. Promotes aviation education in schools.

The Air League 4 Hamilton Place, London W1V 0BQ. Tel: 01 499 6400. Promotes air defence and General Aviation as a civil air arm, encourages youth programmes.

Aircraft Owners & Pilots Association (AOPA) 50A Cambridge Street, London SW1V 4QQ. Tel: 01 834 5631. National and International representative body for General Aviation pilots, aircraft owners and flying training organisations.

Air Transport Operators Association (ATOA) Clembro House, Weydown Road, Haslemere, Surrey GU27 2QE. Tel: (0428) 4804. Organisation for air taxi operators.

Auster Pilots' Club c/o 31 Bradenham Beeches, Walters Ash, High Wycombe HP14 4XW. Organisation for Auster Aircraft owners.

British Aerobatic Association (BAeA) Channings, Little Heath Road, Fontwell, Arundel, W. Sussex. Tel: (0243) 683263. Organising body for aerobatics.

British Aircraft Preservation Council (BAPC) 151 Marshalswick Lane, St. Albans, Hertfordshire. Co-ordinating body for preservation of historic aircraft.

British Balloon & Airship Club Kimberley House, 47 Vaughan Way, Leicester LE1 4SG. Tel: (0533) 531051. Organisation for lighter-than-air flight.

British Gliding Association (BGA) Kimberley House, 47 Vaughan Way, Leicester LE1 4SG. Tel: (0533) 531051. Representative body for gliding in U.K.

British Hang Gliding Association (BHGA) Cranfield Aerodrome, Cranfield, Beds MK3 0AL. Tel: (0234) 751688. Representative body for U.K. hang-gliding activities.

British Helicopter Advisory Board (BHAB) Knowles House, Cromwell Road, Redhill, Surrey RH1 1LW. Tel: (0737) 62371. Promotes and advises on helicopter operations.

British Microlight Aircraft Association (BMAA) New Street, Deddington, Oxford OX5 4SP. Tel: (0869) 38888. Representative body for microlight aircraft flying in U.K.

British Parachute Association (BPA) Kimberley House, 47 Vaughan Way, Leicester LE1 3SG. Tel: (0533) 59635/59778. Representative body for the sport of parachuting.

British Precision Pilots Association (BPPA) 2 Park Avenue, Harpenden, Hertfordshire. Tel: (05827) 65072. Promotes the sport of aerial orienteering.

British Women Pilots' Association (BWPA) 26 Fouberts Place, London W1V 2AL. Promotes training and employment of women in aviation.

Business Aircraft Users Association (BAUA) P.O. Box 29, Wallingford, Oxon OX10 0AG. Tel: (0491) 37903. Represents users of professionally operated company aircraft.

DHC-1 Chipmunk Club c/o Soller, Barnet Road, Arkley, Herts. Organisation for Chipmunk owners.

DH Moth Club c/o 23 Hall Park Hill, Berkhamsted, Herts HP4 2NH. Organisation for owners of DH Moth aircraft.

Flying Farmers Association Ox House, Shobdon, Leominster HR6 9LT. Tel: (05688) 1351. Promotes aviation to Farmers.

Formula Air Racing Association (FARA) c/o The Tiger Club, Redhill Aerodrome, Redhill, Surrey. Tel: (073 782) 2212. Promotes Formula One air racing in the U.K.

General Aviation Manufacturers & Traders Association (GAMTA) 26 High Street, Brill, Aylesbury, Bucks HP18 9ST. Tel: (0844) 238389. U.K. General Aviation trade organisation for all commercial activities.

General Aviation Safety Committee (GASCO) Church House, 33 Church Street, Henley-on-Thames, Oxfordshire RG9 1SE. Tel: (0491) 574476. Organisation fostering greater safety in G.A. operations.

Guild of Air Pilots & Navigators (GAPAN) 30 Eccleston Street, London SW1W 9PY. Tel: 01 730 0471. Livery company of the City of London for all licensed pilots and navigators.

Guild of Aviation Artists 11 Great Spilmans, London SE22 8SZ. Represents aviation artists.

Historic Aircraft Association (HAA) c/o Registration Secretary, 14 Pall Mall, London SW1 5LU. Represents the interests of historic aircraft display pilots.

Lawyers Flying Association Second Floor, 1 Finsbury Avenue, London EC2M 2PJ. Tel: 01 377 9191. Represents the interests of members of the legal profession who are active or interested in aviation.

Popular Flying Association (PFA) Terminal Building, Shoreham Airport, Shoreham-by-Sea, Sussex BN4 5FF. Tel: (07917) 61616. Representative body of amateur aircraft builders.

The Royal Aero Club of the U.K. (RAeC) Kimberley House, 47 Vaughan Way, Leicester LE1 4SG. Tel: (0533) 351051. U.K. National Aero Club, representing the Federation Aeronautique International (FAI), controlling body of all international sporting aviation.

The Royal Aeronautical Society 4 Hamilton Place, London W1V 0BQ. Tel: 01 499 3515/9.

Vintage Aircraft Club c/o 5 North Street, Thame, Oxon. Supporting body for owners and pilots of vintage aircraft.

British Airports Authority London Gatwick Airport, Gatwick, West Sussex RH6 0HZ. Tel: (0293) 517755.

Civil Aviation Authority *Headquarters:* CAA House, 45–59 Kingsway, London WC2B 6TE. Tel: 01 379 7311. *Public Relations:* Ext. 2335/6. *Central Library:* Ext. 2913. *U.K. Register of Civil Aircraft:* Ext. 2202/2206. *Aeronautical Information Service:* Tolcarne Drive, Pinner, Middlesex HA5 2DU. Tel: 01 866 8781. *Printing & Publications Services:* Greville House, 37 Gratton Road, Cheltenham, Glos GL50 2BN. Tel: (0242) 35151. *CAA Scotland:* Aviation House: 1A Traquair Park East, Edinburgh EH12 7BB. Tel: 031 334 0333.

National Air Traffic Services *Headquarters:* CAA House, 45–49 Kingsway, London WC2B 6TE. Tel: 01 379 7311. *Joint Field Headquarters:* Hillingdon House, Uxbridge, Middlesex UB10 0RU. Tel: (0895) 57300.

Safety *CAA Airworthiness Division:* Brabazon House, Redhill, Surrey RH1 1SQ. Tel: (0737) 65966. *CAA Flight Operations Inspectorate:* Aviation House, 129 Kingsway, London WC2B 6NN. Tel: 01 405 6922. *CAA General Aviation Branch:* Aviation House, 129 Kingsway, London WC2B 6NN. Tel: 01 405 6922. *Joint Airmiss Section — Airmiss Reports:* Hillingdon House, Uxbridge, Middlesex UB10 0RU. Tel: (0895) 57324.

Index